David Bez of Salad Pride

SALADLOVE

How to create a lunchtime salad,
every weekday, in 20 minutes or less

Quadrille
PUBLISHING

To my mum.
To my family.

Publishing Director: Jane O'Shea
Creative Director: Helen Lewis
Senior Editor: Céline Hughes
Designer and Photographer: David Bez
Production: Vincent Smith, Aysun Hughes,
   Leonie Kellman, Sasha Hawkes

First published in 2014 by
Quadrille Publishing Limited
Alhambra House
27–31 Charing Cross Road
London WC2H 0LS
www.quadrille.co.uk

Cataloguing in Publication Data: a catalogue record for this
book is available from the British Library.

ISBN: 978 184949 496 0

CONTENTS

INTRODUCTION

THIS IS NOT A COOKBOOK

I'm not a chef; I'm a designer and food lover raised in Milan. This is a book about why I love salads, what inspired me to make a new one every day and how you can do the same. It won't teach you how to cook – it is a collection of salad combinations that I've actually prepared and eaten. I'm not a food stylist or a food photographer but I made these plates of salad for my lunch and photographed them before tucking in. They were made at my desk in my office, when I have just an hour (sometimes half) to get my lunch and eat it, like most people. Sure, there are a lot of things you can buy on the high street, at restaurants (too expensive) or pre-prepared from the supermarket (not as fresh as I would like). I wanted something healthy, fresh, tasty and quick and often that's difficult to find. I like good food and I'm quite fussy about it. I know I'm not alone. For most nine-to-fivers, lunch is a functional moment in the day, merely a way to replenish – and it's rarely a pleasure. I do not see it that way: my Italian genes scream loudly and refuse to surrender to eating any old thing.

Moreover, I don't trust how shops and supermarkets select and process their so-called "healthy" foods. I care about where my ingredients have been sourced and how they have been put together. I don't want them to contain weird chemicals with crazy scientific names. I want to be able to choose something that is truly healthy, not "healthier" or even worse, fake "healthy" like some low-fat but sugar-loaded yoghurts or cereals.

I've been reading a lot about nutrition, eating seasonally, the properties of various ingredients, vegetarianism, veganism, raw veganism, blood pH levels, local farming, organic farming, and so on. As a result, I feel more knowledgeable on many food-related issues (although sometimes I feel more confused than ever – is soy milk good for you or not?!) The basic principle that most people seem to agree on is that we need to eat a lot of grains and fresh fruits and vegetables, not just because it's better for us, but because it's better for the planet as well. It's as simple as that!

I have another simple lunch rule: I want to finish my lunch feeling energised and ready to work. If I feel tired and sleepy, that is not a good meal. On top of that, I always try to buy organic, fairtrade, sustainable and locally sourced as much as I can. Why? I'm a dad, I care about the future of my son, and yes, I know it sounds grandiose, but together, simply by changing our dietary habits, we can all can make an impact, and our choices can give us a better world.

1,000 DAYS OF OFFICE LUNCHES, OR MORE

In order to be able to eat the healthy, fresh food I wanted, I decided to prepare my own lunch every day in the office. I wanted these meals to be something easy enough to prepare at my desk. Mind you, there aren't that many things you can prepare at your desk, especially if you hate the microwave. Yes, I hate the microwave. I have never liked the idea of warming up pre-prepared food in a plastic box. While I love to cook at home, cooking in the office is not practical, so I had to compromise. Some ingredients – the fresh ones – could be brought to the office and refrigerated; others could be prepared in the office with a kettle (or even a hot water dispenser); and others could be brought in pre-cooked (such as last night's dinner leftovers).

I started by doing a weekly shop on Monday morning, buying enough ingredients for the week ahead, plus a little more, just in case. I always looked at what was in season and, depending on my mood, I relied on a mixture of improvisation and planning. And the food that was left over on Friday afternoons I brought home. I kept my fresh ingredients in the communal fridge, taking up a whole shelf (my colleagues probably hate me as a result). I transformed my desk drawer into kitchen storage area, keeping essential tools there like a chopping board, a proper knife, a small salad spinner, a tin opener and some dried ingredients like spices, tinned beans, nuts and dried fruits (some of which I also snacked on during the day).

And every day at lunchtime I turned my desk into a little kitchen countertop, creating temporary havoc – chaotic but controlled. That is, until I started cutting raw beetroot and get my hands all "bloody" just before a big meeting. Now, I wear latex gloves when I'm dealing with that sort of dangerous stuff.

I find myself relaxing quite a lot while I chop and mix, shuck and rinse. My lunch break has become a little zen moment. It's not just a matter of preparing and eating, it's the pleasure of smelling and feeling the ingredients and flavours of the food. There is an interesting mindfulness when you allow yourself to be silent and concentrate on the task at hand. You can also free up your senses, even for just 15 minutes. Preparing food is a very rich sensory experience. There are not just colours and shapes to exploit, but new experiments using unscripted combinations of texture, taste, aroma and visual appeal. I use my imagination to make each lunch break an exciting exploration of as-yet-unexplored food terrains.

As soon as I began making these balanced, nutritious salads, my colleagues were immediately attracted to the idea and kept wanting to tuck into my creations. "What are you preparing there?" they would constantly ask. "What a great smell of basil!" they exclaimed. Everyone was fascinated by my culinary flights of salad fancy. So it occurred to me that they might be of interest to a wider audience and I started to take pictures and post them on a blog. It has now been three years since I began creating a new and different lunch every day. Really! Three years! I can't believe the number of combinations I've created – some extremely delicious, some really good, others… I've learnt a lot along the way and I've definitely honed my skills. It took three years to find the magic formula. Most of all, I wanted to demonstrate that I could make a healthy lunch at my desk but, just as importantly, I wanted what I was eating to be a yummy, sophisticated and complete meal. I believe I have succeeded, but it's up to you to decide.

When I first embarked on the project, I didn't know how to begin. For one thing, I wasn't on a diet. I didn't need to lose weight; I just wanted to eat right and I still wanted plenty of flavours in my meal. So I started with some random tests and quickly realised that what I was doing was making salads. How did I define a salad? Given my office constraints, my lunch had to be a cold dish, made from various cold ingredients, mostly fresh or previously cooked vegetables, topped with a dressing.

I love to use very simple ingredients and I found that the fewer the ingredients, the better the salad; and I liked it best when I was still able to identify each individual ingredient on my plate. Too many elements chopped too finely made the meal taste all the same. For convenience, I was constrained by what was available in any supermarket and what was in season, but I also wanted to use the occasional fancy ingredient – something unusual, unexpected or just a bit more expensive to treat myself, like truffle oil, saffron or caviar.

I tried to come up with rules. More leaves, less meat, more veggies or fruit and less cheese, more beans and fewer carbs, more nuts and less salt. As soon as I created a rule, though, I immediately wanted to change it or disobey it. You'll see how many times I have broken the rules, but it's a good idea, nonetheless, to start with some guidelines and boundaries.

1. Base

2. Vegetables & fruit

3. Protein

4. Toppings

5. Fresh herbs

6. Dressing & spices

1.

2.

3.

4.

5.

6.

HOW TO ASSEMBLE A SALAD

When composing a salad, I divide it into different layers: base, vegetables and fruit, protein, toppings, fresh herbs, and dressings and spices. These are the main ingredients but as you will see, often one (sometimes two) of them is missing. It's up to you to choose what you want to put in it and to enjoy what you are eating. Because these salads are simple assembly jobs, throughout the book I've listed the ingredients that went into each one but no instructions are needed as such.

If you are a strict vegetarian, vegan or "rawist", please check carefully that the ingredients you buy comply with these diets. I've included plenty of cheeses in the vegetarian salads because some vegetarians choose to eat cheese, and because there is a growing number of rennet-free cheeses available, but do replace them if necessary. For raw diets, make sure nuts, dried fruit etc. have been produced within the temperature limitations of strictly raw products.

The base usually takes up to 50% of your salad – in volume not in weight, as leafy greens are usually quite light. It can be made with salad leaves, but also with pasta, grains, potatoes or even veggie 'noodles' like shaved carrots or courgette ribbons.

25% of the salad should be composed of vegetables and/or fruits, preferably fresh and raw, but they can be also be roasted, steamed, boiled or even dried like sun-dried tomatoes, or preserved in olive oil like tomatoes, peppers or aubergines.

On top of this you might add some protein. You can get your proteins from a very broad range of sources, not just from meat – see page 19. In order to have a balanced diet, proteins shouldn't take over your plate but they should provide a bit of additional flavour.

Next, you can use some toppings to boost the overall taste and texture of the salad: for example pickled veggies or olives, croutons or toasted nuts and seeds, but I would say no more than a handful of these (roughly 2 tablespoons).

To top it all, I always love to add some fresh herbs. And finally, I end with the dressing. Never underestimate it. It's like the sauce for the pasta and it can transform your mix of assorted veggies into a feast.

1. THE BASE

Salad leaves are actually the most recognisable element of a salad, i.e. the first association your mind will make as soon as you say the word "salad". There are so many different leaves, from rocket to iceberg (not one of my favourites); from the bitter radicchio to the mild gems of romaine; from baby spinach to red oak leaf lettuce; from tender lamb's lettuce to spicy watercress.

I love their crispness and freshness – so deliciously satisfying. I like to use raw winter leaves as well, such as cabbage, pak choi, kale or chard because they are crunchy and spicy. If you want them to be slightly softer in texture, wash them in warm water or massage them with some lemon juice. Sometimes I like to use veggies, not just leaves, as a base. I like anything that can be chopped finely like cauliflower florets, or shaved into "spaghetti" or ribbons like carrots, courgettes, parsnips, cucumber or asparagus. A vegetable peeler, grater or mandoline will do the job, and it will look very cool too! I've learnt all these ways of preparing vegetables from raw vegan cuisine. Do wash or peel the veggies first, as you prefer.

I love to use grains as well since they are filling, add texture, and offer another delicious element to salads. This is one of the few ingredients I bring from home. When I cook some pasta, rice, quinoa or any other grain for dinner (and that happens quite often), I cook some extra for myself for the next day. I leave it aside to cool, then I store it in the fridge, and usually I add a sprinkle of olive oil to prevent it from becoming sticky. I love white rice but I find salads work better with less sticky, wholewheat varieties like brown, red, black and wild rice. Barley, spelt and quinoa work very well too. And I am mad about couscous. We never ate it in Italy, so it was a fantastic discovery for me, as were all the grains, spices and ingredients of Middle Eastern cuisine. I make couscous all the time in the office. It's so easy, it's like making tea! I take a big tea cup, fill it one-third of the way up with couscous and add a pinch of salt and a dash of olive oil. Then I pour boiling water in, to just cover the couscous, cover the cup with a cloth and leave it to sit for 5–10 minutes. Job done.

2. VEGETABLES & FRUIT

Veggies should take up 25% of your salad, not just because we are advised to eat at least five pieces of fruit and vegetable a day, but because they are good, tasty and full of colour, vitamins, minerals and fibre. I usually try to use two veggies or fruits on my salads, just to have a bit of variety, but I can use more or less. I love big chunks rather than super-fine ones: I relish each ingredient and like to be able to recognise the different pieces in my mouthful of salad.

If I can, I prefer to keep veggies raw, as their distinctive flavour remains intact and they keep all their nutritional value, vitamins and nutrients. Fruits look gorgeous in salads, and they pair up so well with cheese. I like to mix two of them together, which is a very safe option. I also like to mix and match raw veggies with fruits, which can result in very interesting and exotic combinations! Avocado, for instance, can create different effects in a salad, as it can provide firm chunks, or be so yielding and creamy that it acts almost as a dressing.

I don't use cooked fruits in salads. It's not a cake, right? On the other hand, I am very fond of incorporating dried fruits but I'll talk about them later, in the toppings section on page 21. The second best option is to steam the veggies. Usually, I do it the night before as part of my dinner and I keep the leftovers in the fridge until the next day. Another, lengthier option is to roast them. I like to chop the veggies, add a bit of spice, salt and oil and chuck them in a hot oven for 30–40 minutes until golden and soft. You can fry them in a pan or a wok too, but it's something I don't do that often.

My favourite veggies to use raw are cucumbers, peppers, tomatoes, red onions, carrots, celery, courgettes, radishes, beetroots, cauliflower, broccoli, fennel, parsnip, asparagus, green beans and shallots. I've probably left some out!
My favourite veggies to use steamed are butternut squash, artichokes, sweet potatoes, broccoli, asparagus, green beans, peas, Jerusalem artichokes and new potatoes.
My favourite veggies to use roasted are peppers, butternut squash, onions, artichokes, sweet potatoes, broccoli, aubergines, asparagus, green beans, peas, pumpkins, Jerusalem artichokes, new potatoes, shallots and so on.
My favourite fruits to use are avocado, mango, apples, apricots, blackberries, oranges, blueberries, cherries, figs, grapes, melons, watermelon, nectarines, peaches, pears, plums, raspberries, redcurrants and strawberries.

3. PROTEIN

One cup, or 25% of your salad should be dedicated to proteins, which also enhance the flavour of your salad. Don't forget that you can get protein from a wide range of ingredients. Depending on your dietary requirements and your taste, you can get it from meat (chicken, duck, goose, lamb, turkey, beef and pork); seafood (cod , tuna, crab, sole, haddock, herring, lobster, mackerel, prawns, salmon, sardines, scallops, seabass, trout, squid, octopus); eggs; cheese (mozzarella, ricotta, Parmesan, brie, cottage cheese, goats' cheese, Cheddar, gorgonzola, other blue cheese, halloumi, gouda, Manchego); soy products such as tofu; pulses (lentils, pinto, kidney, black beans, cannellini beans, broad beans, mung beans, chickpeas); grains (quinoa, wheat, couscous, rice, amaranth, barley, rye, oats, buckwheat); or even nuts and seeds (hemp, almonds, Brazil nuts, hazelnuts, walnuts, cashew nuts, pine nuts, pistachios, pumpkin seeds, sesame seeds). Surprised? I often use two different types in my salad – a nut and a cheese, a seed and a fish, a cheese and some meat.

Occasionally I go for raw fish, such as salmon or tuna. This is sometimes called sashimi fish, and you should buy it from a reliable fishmonger and tell him or her that you plan to eat it raw, so that you know you're getting the freshest and best-quality fish. A note on sustainability: I only buy fish and prawns if I know they have been responsibly sourced. I don't want to contribute to the depletion of fish stocks, and we all have a responsibility to care about where our food comes from and how it's been acquired. For more information, visit the Marine Conservation Society at www.fishonline.org and www.mcsuk.org. The same principle applies to all ingredients made from animal products (e.g. eggs, cheese and meat); I would recommend you buy the best quality you can afford and that it's free-range, organic and fairtrade where possible.

I always store nuts and leftover tinned ingredients in a well sealed container in my drawer or the fridge where necessary (I always fear mice!) I would keep the amount of protein ingredients below the 25% mark, otherwise your plate becomes chicken with a salad on the side, instead of salad with a bit of chicken.

4. TOPPINGS

I call toppings all those salty, nutty and sweet extra ingredients you need just a tablespoon or two of to brighten the overall combination of your meal.

Nuts and seeds are not just a great source of protein, they taste incredibly good and are full of good fats, and they add extra crunchiness to the whole dish. Some nuts and seeds are better soaked overnight, especially almonds. Others are amazing toasted, like sesame seeds, pumpkin seeds, cashews and pine nuts. Some of my favourites are hemp, almonds, pecan nuts, hazelnuts, walnuts, cashew nuts, pine nuts, pistachios, pumpkin seeds, sesame seeds, poppy seeds, and linseeds, to name a few.

I love to use pickled veggies like olives, capers, gherkins, baby onions and so on, as they boost the savouriness of the salad. Alternatively I like to use dried fruits like unsulphured apricots, dates, raisins, prunes, blueberries to enhance the sweet accents.

5. FRESH HERBS

I always try to add a handful of fresh herbs like basil, chives, coriander, dill, mint, oregano, parsley, rosemary, sage, tarragon, thyme (or even sprouted beans) in my salads. They are an essential part of all my recipes; they are the touch that makes a boring salad a rich and synesthetic experience with their amazing smell and taste. I've learnt this from Yotam Ottolenghi, who is a salad master! I love to buy pots of fresh herbs, especially basil, parsley and mint which last longer and look good as well. Luckily my desk is by the window…

6. DRESSING & SPICES

The dressing is where the real magic happens, and the stage at which a salad comes to life. In all your dressings you want to balance some sweet oiliness (oil or nuts), some sourness (vinegar, soy sauce or citrus juices) and bit of saltiness and spice. Leafy salads should only be dressed just before serving since the dressing will "cook" your leaves and they will become dark and soggy if left too long. Grain and cabbage salads are the opposite and become better when you leave them to absorb the dressing.

Dried herbs, spices and other ingredients (like basil, chives, coriander, dill, mint, oregano, parsley, rosemary, sage, tarragon, thyme, truffles, nori seaweed, turmeric, curry powder, saffron, fennel, nutmeg, cardamom, cumin, pepper, cayenne pepper, bay, cinnamon, mustard seeds, garlic, wasabi, ginger, galangal, kaffir lime leaves, marjoram, paprika, sumac) play an important role in the direction you want your salad to go. It's not just about salt and pepper. There are a lot of fantastic spices that can boost your dressing. Don't be too generous as you will taste them much more keenly than you would in a cooked dish. Half a teaspoon is usually enough.

Spices are also really good at complementing the seasons. Spices and herbs are great in the summer when it's hot, as they can cool you down: mint, basil, fennel, coriander and tarragon all work well, as they are fresh. Conversely, I use spices in dressings to warm myself up. Black pepper, cayenne, cinnamon, ginger, horseradish (or wasabi), mustard, chilli and paprika are some of my favourites.

There are many different types of dressings, but I divide them into three categories: oily (vinaigrette-style), creamy and pesto. On the following pages are some of my most-loved ones, and you can choose any of these, or you can simply follow the dressing suggestions given in each salad recipe. You either just mix them together with a fork or whisk, or occasionally you need to blend the ingredients together – I have a tiny little blender (designed for baby purées) that I use.

VINAIGRETTE-STYLE DRESSINGS

CLASSIC ITALIAN

*Mix 2 tbsp extra virgin olive oil, 1 tsp balsamic vinegar
and a pinch of salt and pepper*

WASABI & SOY SAUCE

*Mix 1 tbsp toasted sesame oil, 1 tbsp dark soy sauce,
1 tsp wasabi powder and 1 tsp rapeseed oil*

CITRUS

*Mix 2 tbsp extra virgin olive oil, 1 tsp orange juice,
1 tsp lemon juice and a pinch of salt*

LEMON ZEST

*Mix 2 tbsp extra virgin olive oil, 2 tsp lemon juice,
a pinch of salt and a sprinkle of grated lemon zest*

CHILLI

*Mix 2 tbsp extra virgin olive oil, 1 tsp cider vinegar,
a pinch of salt and 1–2 pinches of chilli powder*

TRUFFLE

*Mix 2 tbsp extra virgin olive oil, 1 tsp truffle-infused
olive oil, 1 tsp balsamic vinegar and a pinch of salt
and pepper*

PESTO DRESSINGS

CLASSIC PESTO

Blend together 2 tbsp extra virgin olive oil, a pinch of salt and pepper, 1 handful of fresh basil leaves, 1 tbsp pine nuts, 1 tbsp grated Parmesan and ¼ garlic clove

OLIVE TAPENADE

Blend together 2 tbsp extra virgin olive oil, 1 tsp cider vinegar, a pinch of salt and pepper and 2 tbsp pitted black or green olives

ARTICHOKE PESTO

Blend together 2 tsp extra virgin olive oil, 1 tsp artichoke paste, 1 tsp cider vinegar and a pinch of salt

RASPBERRY PESTO

Blend together 2 tbsp extra virgin olive oil, 1 tsp lemon juice, a pinch of salt and pepper and a handful of raspberries

RAW GREEN PESTO

Blend together 2 tbsp extra virgin olive oil, a pinch of salt and pepper, a handful of fresh herbs (e.g. basil, coriander, parsley), 1 tbsp nuts (e.g. pine nuts, cashew nuts, walnuts, almonds, pistachios) and 1 tbsp water

TOMATO PESTO

Blend together 1 tsp sun-dried tomatoes, 1 tbsp pine nuts, 2 tsp extra virgin olive oil, 1 tsp cider vinegar and a pinch of salt and pepper

CREAMY DRESSINGS

NUT & LEMON

Blend together 2 tsp extra virgin olive oil, 1 tsp lemon juice, a pinch of salt, 2 tsp nuts (e.g. almonds, cashew nuts, walnuts) and 1 tsp water

TOASTED SESAME

Blend together 2 tbsp extra virgin olive oil, 1 tsp cider vinegar, 1 tsp tahini, a pinch of salt and 2 tbsp toasted sesame seeds

THAI CURRY

Blend together 2 tbsp soya cream, 1 tbsp desiccated coconut and 1 tsp Thai green curry paste

VEGAN COCONUT & GINGER

Blend together 2 tbsp soya cream, 1 tsp coconut water or milk, 2 tbsp desiccated coconut and 1 tsp ground ginger

ENGLISH MUSTARD

Mix 2 tbsp extra virgin olive oil, 1 tbsp mayonnaise, 1 tsp English mustard and a pinch of salt

CREAM & SPICES

Mix 1 tsp ground spice (e.g. smoked paprika, chilli, cumin, ginger, turmeric), 2 tbsp single cream and a pinch of salt

HOUMOUS

Mix 2 tbsp extra virgin olive oil, 2 tbsp houmous, 1 tsp lemon juice, a pinch of salt and pepper and 2 pinches of smoked paprika

RAW NUT & AGAVE

Blend together 2 tbsp extra virgin olive oil, 2 tbsp cashew nuts, a pinch of salt, 1 tsp water and 1 tsp agave nectar

SAFFRON MAYO

Mix 2 tbsp mayonnaise, 1 tsp cider vinegar, a pinch of saffron threads and a pinch of salt

FRENCH MUSTARD

Blend together 2 tbsp extra virgin olive oil, 1 tsp cider vinegar, a pinch of salt and pepper, 1 tsp single cream and 1 tsp wholegrain Dijon mustard

TARTARE

Blend together 1 tsp capers, 2 tsp extra virgin olive oil, 1 tsp lemon juice, 2 tbsp natural yoghurt, a pinch of salt and pepper and 1 tbsp fresh parsley leaves

RAW PINE NUT "MAYO"

Blend together 2 tsp extra virgin olive oil, 2 tsp pine nuts, a pinch of salt, 1 tsp water and 1 tsp ground turmeric

MY TOOLS

You can't have a whole kitchen for you in the office, but you need a series of basic tools to be able to create a good, fresh salad. First you need a chopping board and a knife; without those it is quite hard to function effectively. I always suggest having a proper kitchen knife on hand. It makes the chopping easier, quicker and more precise.

One of my favourite tools is the vegetable peeler. Use it to peel veggies and fruits, of course, but also learn to use it to shave into ribbons or flakes hard cheeses like Parmesan and Pecorino or veggies like courgettes, cucumber, carrots and parsnips. If you want to simulate "spaghetti", use a julienne peeler and the ribbons magically become thinner strips.

Another essential tool is the salad spinner, a compact version of which fits in my desk drawer. I always recommend that you wash even pre-washed packed lettuce. Wet salad bags are bacteria heaven! I use a little bowl or jar that I use to mix dressings. In the beginning I had measuring spoons, but now I don't use them any more as my eye is trained enough to gauge size and weight with a glance. Like my mum used to say: "you need enough of that ingredient", to which I would reply "how much is enough?" And she used to say "when it's enough, you'll see it, you'll know it". She used to cook divinely.

I always have a collection of airtight boxes in different sizes. I often use less than a packet of cheese, meat or ham in any one salad and store the leftovers for the next day. I try to plan ahead when I go food shopping. For example, I might buy 100 g cheese to use in at least two recipes over the next few days.

Other tools I have that you might like to equip yourself with: tin opener, sieve, rubber gloves (for chopping beetroot or red cabbage!), pestle and mortar, grater, scissors. I have them all, and my drawer is almost exploding. I have a sprout germinator, too, and everything needed for washing my plate and utensils at the end of lunch.

A YEAR OF SALADS

I've learnt a lot in my journey creating daily lunch salads, a journey which has included some failures but mostly successes. I believe more than ever that salads are a great meal. For three years, I succeeded in creating a lunch at my desk every single day. I've discovered how good my own rich, gorgeous and tasty salads can be, and how easy to prepare. At the end of it all, I am just as much in love with salads as when I started. It really hurts me when I see them being treated simply as a sad and unsexy little side dish, or a prelude to the main event. Salads can be beautiful and bright, healthy and tasty, a fulfilling and complete meal. In conducting this experiment, I've tried to give salads and healthy eating a new and more appealing image.

I know that I am not alone: I've seen a lot of people changing their diets and embracing healthier habits around me in my office, in London and around the world. The perception about salads and healthy food has changed. I've seen colleagues of mine creating Salad Clubs, preparing their fresh salads at their desks or in communal areas. At the same time, by eating these yummy, vitamin- and mineral-rich creations, I feel I've changed my body, my appearance and my point of view about food in general. After these days, weeks, months and years of creating salads, I love food now more than ever, and I've never been so enthusiastic about salads. Eating healthily was never meant to be boring or painful; it should and can be a delicious treat to ourselves. In this book I've decided to represent the best examples of my years of salad exploration: the most interesting and outrageous, the most innovative and successful.

The recipes in this book are real meals, photographed just a few seconds before being devoured. They were all assembled in no more than 20 minutes (and some required ingredients to be pre-cooked, either by you the night before or by a deli or supermarket). They are divided by season and cover five different dietary requirements – raw, vegan, vegetarian, pescatarian and omnivore.

There is a salad for everyone, for any time, any mood and any budget. I've also added an "alternative" to each one to help you convert it for a different diet, or just to make it lighter or richer depending on your mood. I hope I can fire your imagination and inspire you to create different, new and even more interesting combinations. Buon appetito!

SUMMER

VEGETARIAN

RAW
ALTERNATIVE
*Replace the mozzarella
with 1 ripe avocado
and ¼ red onion*

MOZZARELLA, CHERRY TOMATOES & SPINACH

For the salad, assemble:

50 g baby spinach
200 g cherry tomatoes, halved
100 g mozzarella, chopped
handful of fresh basil leaves

For the dressing, mix:

1 tbsp extra virgin olive oil
1 tsp balsamic vinegar
pinch of salt and pepper
pinch of dried oregano

CRABMEAT, CHERRY TOMATOES & WATERCRESS

For the salad, assemble:

50 g watercress
100 g cherry tomatoes, halved
50 g cooked crabmeat
handful of pine nuts
handful of fresh flat-leaf parsley leaves

For the dressing, mix:

1 tbsp extra virgin olive oil
1 tsp balsamic vinegar
pinch of salt and pepper

RAW

VEGETARIAN ALTERNATIVE
Add 100 g feta or goats' cheese

BLACK GRAPES, MELON & HEMP CREAM

For the salad, assemble:

1 little gem lettuce
100 g honeydew or galia melon, chopped
handful of black grapes
1 tbsp shelled hemp seeds
handful of fresh mint leaves

For the dressing, blend together:

1 tbsp extra virgin olive oil
1 tsp lemon juice
pinch of salt and pepper
handful of shelled hemp seeds

RAW ALTERNATIVE

Replace the yoghurt with the Raw Nut & Agave dressing on page 27, made with almonds

STRAWBERRIES, MELON & ALMONDS

For the salad, assemble:

50 g red oak leaf lettuce
100 g strawberries, hulled and chopped
100 g charentais or cantaloupe melon, chopped
handful of almonds, chopped
handful of fresh mint leaves

For the dressing, mix:

50 g natural yoghurt
1 tbsp extra virgin olive oil
pinch of salt and pepper

PESCATARIAN

VEGAN
ALTERNATIVE
*Replace the salmon with
tinned black beans, and
add white pepper*

HONEY-ROASTED SALMON, FENNEL & SPINACH

For the salad, assemble:

50 g baby spinach
½ fennel bulb, thinly sliced
100 g cherry tomatoes, halved
50 g honey-roasted salmon, flaked
handful of pumpkin seeds
handful of fresh flat-leaf parsley leaves

For the dressing, mix:

1 tbsp extra virgin olive oil
1 tsp lemon juice
pinch of salt and pepper

PARMA HAM, PARMESAN & CHERRY TOMATOES

For the salad, assemble:

50 g rocket
150 g cherry tomatoes, halved
50 g Parma ham, roughly shredded
50 g Parmesan shavings

For the dressing, mix:

1 tbsp extra virgin olive oil
1 tsp balsamic vinegar
pinch of salt and pepper

RAW

OMNIVORE ALTERNATIVE
Add 50 g chorizo or pastrami

PURPLE CARROT, RED PEPPER & CHILLI PESTO

For the salad, assemble:

2 small purple (or orange) carrots, shaved into
* ribbons with a vegetable peeler*
½ red romano pepper, diced
handful of fresh mint leaves

For the dressing, blend together:

1 tbsp extra virgin olive oil
1 tsp cider vinegar
pinch of salt and pepper
½ red chilli, chopped
handful of cashew nuts (soaked overnight
* if preferred)*

SWEET POTATO, RED CABBAGE & CHERRY TOMATOES

For the salad, assemble:

100 g red cabbage, finely shredded
½ pre-baked sweet potato, peeled and chopped
100 g cherry tomatoes, quartered
2 spring onions, finely chopped
1 tbsp sesame seeds

For the dressing, mix:

1 tbsp extra virgin olive oil
1 tsp lemon juice
pinch of salt and pepper
2 tbsp vegan houmous

VEGAN

VEGETARIAN ALTERNATIVE

Add some crumbled cheese, such as goats' cheese, feta or Pecorino

CHICKPEAS, COUSCOUS & CHERRY TOMATOES

For the salad, assemble:

100 g cooked couscous
100 g tinned chickpeas
100 g cherry tomatoes, quartered
1 tsp toasted sesame seeds
handful of pitted black olives, halved
handful of fresh flat-leaf parsley leaves

For the dressing, mix:

1 tbsp extra virgin olive oil
1 tsp cider vinegar
pinch of salt and pepper

OMNIVORE

VEGAN
ALTERNATIVE
*Replace the spicy roasted
chicken with 100 g
steamed green beans*

CHICKEN, NEW POTATOES & CHERRY TOMATOES

For the salad, assemble:

50 g rocket
100 g cherry tomatoes, halved
100 g pre-roasted new potatoes, halved
50 g pre-roasted spicy chicken, chopped
handful of fresh flat-leaf parsley leaves

For the dressing, mix:

1 tbsp extra virgin olive oil
1 tsp balsamic vinegar
pinch of salt and pepper

VEGAN

VEGETARIAN ALTERNATIVE
Add 50 g natural yoghurt

PEAS & ROASTED SWEET POTATO & AUBERGINE

For the salad, assemble:

100 g pre-cooked brown basmati rice
50 g pre-steamed peas
100 g pre-roasted sweet potato, chopped
½ cubed and pre-roasted aubergine
handful of cashew nuts
handful of fresh coriander leaves

For the dressing, mix:

1 tbsp extra virgin olive oil
1 tsp cider vinegar
pinch of salt and pepper
2 pinches of curry powder

OMINVORE ALTERNATIVE

Replace the prawns with 50 g roasted chicken

PRAWNS, BABY CORN & SUGAR SNAP PEAS

For the salad, assemble:

100 g pre-cooked brown short-grain rice
50 g raw (or lightly pre-steamed) baby corn
50 g raw (or lightly pre-steamed) sugar snap peas
handful of fresh coriander leaves
handful of pre-cooked prawns

For the dressing, blend together:

2 tbsp soya cream
1 tsp coconut water or milk
2 tbsp desiccated coconut
2 pinches of chilli flakes
pinch of salt

VEGETARIAN

VEGAN
ALTERNATIVE
*Replace the Parmesan
with more wholewheat
croutons and green
beans*

GREEN BEANS, PARMESAN & PINE NUTS

For the salad, assemble:

50 g rocket
50 g pre-steamed green beans
50 g Parmesan shavings
handful of pine nuts
handful of wholewheat croutons
handful of fresh basil leaves
bunch of garlic sprouts

For the dressing, mix:

1 tbsp extra virgin olive oil
1 tsp balsamic vinegar
pinch of salt and pepper

CRABMEAT, AVOCADO, NORI & CUCUMBER

For the salad, assemble:

50 g watercress
1 avocado, chopped
100 g cucumber, chopped
50 g cooked crabmeat
1 sheet of nori (toasted seaweed), thinly sliced
1 tsp toasted sesame seeds

For the dressing, mix:

1 tbsp sunflower oil
1 tsp light soy sauce
pinch of salt and pepper
pinch of wasabi powder

VEGAN ALTERNATIVE
Replace the chicken with celery, and the blue cheese with 100 g tinned black lentils or black beans

CHICKEN, BLUE CHEESE & CHERRY TOMATOES

For the salad, assemble:

50 g rocket
handful of cherry tomatoes, quartered
50 g roasted chicken, chopped
50 g blue cheese, chopped

For the dressing, mix:

1 tbsp extra virgin olive oil
1 tsp balsamic vinegar
pinch of salt
pinch of chilli flakes

VEGAN

OMNIVORE
ALTERNATIVE
*Add 50 g roasted
chicken*

NEW POTATOES, GREEN BEANS & BLACK OLIVES

For the salad, assemble:

100 g chopped and pre-steamed new potatoes
50 g pre-steamed green beans
100 g cherry tomatoes, halved
handful of pitted black olives
½ very small red onion, thinly sliced

For the dressing, blend together:

2 handfuls of fresh basil leaves
2 tsp extra virgin olive oil
handful of pine nuts
¼ garlic clove
1 tsp cider vinegar

BLACK LENTILS, COUSCOUS & PECORINO

For the salad, assemble:

100 g cooked couscous
50 g tinned black lentils
30 g Pecorino shavings
3–4 fresh chive flowers (or a bunch of snipped chives)
bunch of fresh flat-leaf parsley leaves

For the dressing, mix:

1 tbsp artichoke paste (or handful of blended marinated artichoke hearts)
1 tbsp extra virgin olive oil
1 tsp balsamic vinegar
pinch of salt and pepper

VEGAN

RAW ALTERNATIVE
Replace the croutons with some nuts or seeds, or just omit them; use raw olives

CHERRY TOMATOES, BLACK OLIVES & BORAGE FLOWERS

For the salad, assemble:

50 g mixed salad leaves (e.g. watercress, red chard
*   and lamb's lettuce)*
100 g cherry tomatoes, halved
½ small cucumber, chopped
2 spring onions, chopped
handful of pitted black olives, halved
handful of croutons
handful of pine nuts
handful of borage flowers

For the dressing, mix:

1 tbsp extra virgin olive oil
1 tsp cider vinegar
pinch of salt and pepper

RAW ALTERNATIVE

Replace the feta with a handful of cashew nuts, 1 tsp capers and ½ small red onion

FETA, WATERMELON & FENNEL

For the salad, assemble:

50 g rocket
100 g watermelon, deseeded and chopped
½ fennel bulb, thinly sliced
handful of pomegranate seeds
50 g feta, chopped
handful of pumpkin seeds
handful of fresh dill fronds

For the dressing, mix:

1 tbsp extra virgin olive oil
1 tsp lemon juice
pinch of salt and pepper

RAW

VEGETARIAN
ALTERNATIVE
*Add 50 g cheese,
such as goats' cheese
or cottage cheese*

CHICORY, STRAWBERRIES & FENNEL

For the salad, assemble:

1 head of red chicory, thinly sliced
½ small fennel bulb, thinly sliced
100 g strawberries, hulled and chopped
1 tbsp pumpkin seeds
handful of fresh mint leaves

For the dressing, mix:

1 tbsp extra virgin olive oil
1 tsp lemon juice
pinch of salt and pepper

VEGAN ALTERNATIVE
Add a handful of croutons to the chopped tomatoes and leave them to soak for 10 minutes

COURGETTE, CHERRY TOMATOES & AVOCADO

For the salad, assemble:

*1 courgette, shaved into ribbons with
  a vegetable peeler*
*100 g black (or regular) cherry tomatoes,
  quartered*
1 avocado, chopped
1 tsp shelled hemp seeds
handful of fresh chives, snipped

For the dressing, mix:

1 tbsp extra virgin olive oil
1 tsp balsamic vinegar
pinch of salt and pepper

PARMA HAM, MELON & CROUTONS

For the salad, assemble:

50 g rocket
50 g Parma ham, roughly shredded
handful of croutons
handful of fresh chives, snipped
100 g charentais or canteloupe melon, chopped

For the dressing, mix:

1 tbsp extra virgin olive oil
1 tsp balsamic vinegar
pinch of salt and pepper

VEGETARIAN

VEGAN
ALTERNATIVE
*Replace the cottage
cheese with soya cream*

COTTAGE CHEESE, PEAS & CUCUMBER

For the salad, assemble:

50 g rocket and baby watercress
50 g pre-steamed peas
50 g cucumber, chopped
50 g cottage cheese
2 spring onions, finely chopped

For the dressing, mix:

1 tbsp extra virgin olive oil
1 tsp cider vinegar
pinch of salt and pepper

ANCHOVIES, CUCUMBER, RED PEPPER & BLACK OLIVES

For the salad, assemble:

100 g cucumber, shredded with a julienne peeler
½ red romano pepper, diced
50 g marinated anchovies
handful of pitted black olives, halved
handful of pine nuts
handful of fresh flat-leaf parsley leaves

For the dressing, mix:

1 tbsp extra virgin olive oil
1 tsp cider vinegar
pinch of salt and pepper

BRESAOLA, NECTARINE & CASHEW NUTS

For the salad, assemble:

50 g mixed salad leaves
2 nectarines, cut into wedges
50 g bresaola (air-dried beef), thinly sliced
handful of cashew nuts
handful of fresh mint leaves

For the dressing, mix:

1 tbsp extra virgin olive oil
1 tsp balsamic vinegar
pinch of salt and pepper

OAK-SMOKED CHEDDAR, PEACHES & BLUEBERRIES

For the salad, assemble:

*50 g mixed baby salad leaves (e.g. chard, spinach and
red oak leaf lettuce)*
2 small peaches, cut into wedges
handful of blueberries
50 g oak-smoked Cheddar, chopped
handful of walnuts, chopped
handful of fresh mint leaves

For the dressing, mix:

1 tbsp extra virgin olive oil
1 tsp balsamic vinegar
pinch of salt and pepper

VEGETARIAN
ALTERNATIVE
*Replace the smoked
ham with tinned beans
or chickpeas and add
more tomatoes*

SMOKED HAM, SCAMORZA & PISTACHIOS

For the salad, assemble:

*60 g mixed salad leaves (e.g. watercress, red oak leaf
  lettuce and rocket)*
100 g cherry tomatoes, halved
50 g smoked ham, thinly sliced
50 g scamorza (smoked cheese), cubed
handful of pistachios

For the dressing, mix:

1 tbsp extra virgin olive oil
1 tsp balsamic vinegar
pinch of salt and pepper

GOATS' CHEESE, RED PEPPER & PINE NUTS

For the salad, assemble:

50 g rocket
¹/₂ red pepper, chopped
50 g firm goats' cheese, chopped
handful of pine nuts

For the dressing, mix:

1 tbsp extra virgin olive oil
1 tsp balsamic vinegar
pinch of salt and pepper
1 tbsp Tomato Pesto (page 25)

VEGAN

RAW
ALTERNATIVE
*Replace the houmous
with a raw houmous-style
dip or a ripe avocado*

RED PEPPER, WATERCRESS & PINE NUTS

For the salad, assemble:

60 g watercress
1 red romano pepper, finely chopped
handful of pine nuts
bunch of fresh chives, snipped

For the dressing, mix:

1 tbsp extra virgin olive oil
1 tsp balsamic vinegar
pinch of salt and pepper
1 tbsp vegan red pepper houmous

RAW

OMNIVORE
ALTERNATIVE
*Add 100 g roasted
chicken or turkey,
pastrami or smoked
ham*

RED & YELLOW PEPPERS, COURGETTE & RAISINS

For the salad, assemble:

1 courgette, shaved into ribbons with a vegetable peeler
½ red romano pepper, thinly sliced
½ yellow romano pepper, thinly sliced
handful of raisins
handful of pine nuts
handful of fresh chives, snipped

For the dressing, mix:

1 tbsp extra virgin olive oil
1 tsp cider vinegar
pinch of salt and pepper

CHORIZO, GREEN OLIVES & WHOLEWHEAT PASTA

For the salad, assemble:

100 g pre-cooked wholewheat penne
100 g cherry tomatoes, halved
50 g chorizo, chopped
handful of pitted green olives
2 spring onions, thinly sliced
handful of fresh flat-leaf parsley leaves

For the dressing, mix:

1 tbsp extra virgin olive oil
1 tsp balsamic vinegar
pinch of salt and pepper
2 pinches of chilli flakes

ROASTED PEPPERS, CHICKPEAS & BARLEY

For the salad, assemble:

100 g pre-cooked barley
1 chopped and pre-roasted red and/or yellow pepper
100 g tinned chickpeas
handful of pitted black olives
handful of fresh flat-leaf parsley leaves

For the dressing, mix:

1 tbsp extra virgin olive oil
1 tsp balsamic vinegar
pinch of salt and pepper

PESCATARIAN

VEGAN
ALTERNATIVE
*Replace the salmon with
100 g tinned chickpeas or
cannellini beans*

ROASTED SALMON, SPELT, COURGETTE & RED PEPPER

For the salad, assemble:

1 courgette, shaved into ribbons with a vegetable peeler
1 red pepper, sliced
50 g pre-cooked spelt, barley or brown basmati rice
50 g roasted salmon, flaked
handful of fresh flat-leaf parsley leaves

For the dressing, mix:

1 tbsp extra virgin olive oil
1 tsp cider vinegar
pinch of salt and pepper

ROASTED AUBERGINE, PEPPERS & COURGETTE

For the salad, assemble:

*½ small courgette, shaved into ribbons with a
   vegetable peeler*
½ small sliced and pre-roasted aubergine
handful of marinated peppers from a jar
1 tsp crispy onions
bunch of fresh chives, snipped

For the dressing, mix:

1 tbsp extra virgin olive oil
1 tsp balsamic vinegar
pinch of salt and pepper

VEGAN

OMNIVORE
ALTERNATIVE
*Add some roasted
chicken or a handful of
cooked prawns*

GREEN BEANS, RED PEPPER, WILD RICE & CHILLI

For the salad, assemble:

150 g pre-cooked wild rice
100 g pre-steamed green beans
½ red pepper, sliced
2 spring onions, thinly sliced
½ small red chilli, finely chopped
handful of fresh baby coriander and red amaranth leaves

For the dressing, mix:

2 cm fresh ginger, peeled and grated
2 tsp sweet white miso
2 tsp oat cream

OMNIVORE

VEGAN ALTERNATIVE
Replace the chicken with 100 g tinned black or aduki beans, or black lentils

COUSCOUS & ROASTED CHICKEN & VEGETABLES

For the salad, assemble:

100 g cooked couscous
50 g pre-roasted chicken breast, chopped
100 g pre-roasted vegetables (e.g. ½ aubergine, ½ red pepper and ½ yellow pepper)
1 tsp toasted pine nuts
handful of fresh flat-leaf parsley leaves

For the dressing, mix:

1 tbsp extra virgin olive oil
1 tsp balsamic vinegar
pinch of salt and pepper
pinch of dried marjoram

RAW

VEGETARIAN ALTERNATIVE
Add some Parmesan and dress the salad with balsamic vinegar glaze

BROCCOLI, STRAWBERRIES & BLUEBERRIES

For the salad, assemble:

80 g mixed baby salad leaves (e.g. chard, watercress and red oak leaf lettuce)
30 g broccoli florets, chopped
handful of strawberries, hulled and quartered
handful of blueberries
handful of hazelnuts, chopped

For the dressing, mix:

1 tbsp extra virgin olive oil
1 tsp lemon juice
pinch of salt and pepper

RAW
ALTERNATIVE
Replace the cottage cheese with Raw Nut & Agave dressing (page 27); use untoasted pumpkin seeds

COTTAGE CHEESE, BLUEBERRIES & SPINACH

For the salad, assemble:

30 g rocket
30 g baby spinach
50 g blueberries
100 g cottage cheese
handful of toasted pumpkin seeds
bunch of fresh chives, snipped

For the dressing, mix:

1 tbsp extra virgin olive oil
1 tsp balsamic vinegar
pinch of salt and pepper

RAW

PESCATARIAN ALTERNATIVE

Add a handful of cooked prawns or 50 g tinned tuna (preserved in water)

RED CABBAGE, COURGETTE, AVOCADO & WALNUTS

For the salad, assemble:

100 g red cabbage, finely shredded
1 small courgette, chopped
1 avocado, chopped
handful of walnuts, chopped
handful of fresh chives, snipped

For the dressing, mix:

1 tbsp extra virgin olive oil
1 tsp lemon juice
pinch of salt and pepper

SQUID, RED CABBAGE, CARROT & BLACK OLIVES

For the salad, assemble:

100 g red cabbage, finely shredded
1 small carrot, shaved into ribbons with a
    vegetable peeler
handful of cherry tomatoes, chopped
handful of pitted black olives, halved
50 g pre-cooked squid, chopped
1 tsp toasted sesame seeds
bunch of fresh chives, snipped

For the dressing, mix:

1 tbsp extra virgin olive oil
1 tsp lemon juice
pinch of salt and pepper
pinch of chilli flakes

RAW

OMNIVORE ALTERNATIVE
Add a handful of chorizo slices and toast the pine nuts

COURGETTE, NASTURTIUMS & WILD ROCKET

For the salad, assemble:

50 g mixed wild salad leaves (e.g. watercress and rocket)
1 courgette, chopped
2 purple (or regular) spring onions, finely chopped
handful of pine nuts
handful of edible red nasturtium flowers

For the dressing, blend together:

1 tbsp extra virgin olive oil
1 tsp lemon juice
pinch of salt and pepper
1 small chilli, chopped

OMNIVORE

RAW ALTERNATIVE
Replace the chicken with a handful of bean sprouts; omit the toasted sesame oil; use fresh ginger

ROASTED CHICKEN, SUGAR SNAP PEAS & NASTURTIUMS

For the salad, assemble:

50 g wild rocket
100 g sugar snap peas or mangetout
100 g pre-roasted chicken breast, chopped
handful of pine nuts
handful of fresh coriander leaves
handful of edible red nasturtium flowers

For the dressing, mix:

1 tbsp extra virgin olive oil
1 tsp lime juice
1 tsp toasted sesame oil
pinch of salt
pinch of ground ginger

PRAWNS, BABY CORN, TOMATOES & CHILLI

For the salad, assemble:

50 g rocket
1 tomato, chopped
100 g pre-steamed baby corn
handful of pre-cooked prawns
handful of pumpkin seeds
1 small red chilli, finely chopped
handful of fresh coriander leaves

For the dressing, mix:

1 tbsp extra virgin olive oil
1 tsp cider vinegar
pinch of salt and pepper

SUN-DRIED TOMATOES, CORN & LETTUCE

For the salad, assemble:

60 g baby red oak leaf lettuce
½ fresh corn cob, shucked
6 sun-dried tomatoes, chopped
handful of pumpkin seeds
handful of fresh chives, snipped

For the dressing, mix:

1 tbsp extra virgin olive oil
1 tsp cider vinegar
pinch of salt and pepper

OMNIVORE

VEGAN
ALTERNATIVE
*Replace the chorizo
with more black beans
and 2 pinches of
chilli flakes*

CHORIZO, SPELT, COURGETTE & BLACK BEANS

For the salad, assemble:

1 courgette, shredded with a julienne peeler
50 g pre-cooked spelt
100 g cherry tomatoes, halved
50 g tinned black beans
handful of pine nuts
50 g chorizo, chopped
2 spring onions, chopped

For the dressing, mix:

1 tbsp extra virgin olive oil
1 tsp balsamic vinegar
pinch of salt and pepper

VEGAN

VEGETARIAN
ALTERNATIVE
*Add 50 g Gouda,
Ossau-iraty or other
medium-soft cheese*

KIDNEY BEANS, WILD RICE & AVOCADO

For the salad, assemble:

100 g pre-cooked mixed brown, wild and red rice
100 g tinned kidney beans
½ avocado, chopped
handful of cherry tomatoes, halved
½ small red onion, finely chopped
handful of fresh flat-leaf parsley leaves

For the dressing, mix:

1 tbsp extra virgin olive oil
1 tsp cider vinegar
pinch of salt and pepper

SQUID, OCTOPUS, COUSCOUS & PEAS

For the salad, assemble:

100 g pre-cooked giant Palestinian couscous
50 g pre-boiled peas
100 g cherry tomatoes, quartered
50 g mixed marinated squid and octopus antipasti

For the dressing, mix:

1 tbsp extra virgin olive oil
1 tsp cider vinegar
pinch salt and pepper
pinch of saffron threads

VEGETARIAN

RAW
ALTERNATIVE
*Replace the Parmesan
with a handful of
walnuts*

STRAWBERRIES, PARMESAN & RED CHICORY

For the salad, assemble:

1 small head of red chicory
150 g strawberries, hulled and quartered
50 g Parmesan shavings
handful of pine nuts
bunch of fresh chives, snipped

For the dressing, mix:

1 tbsp extra virgin olive oil
1 tsp balsamic vinegar
pinch of salt and pepper

RAW

OMNIVORE
ALTERNATIVE
*Add 50 g roasted
chicken*

YELLOW PEPPER, BROCCOLI, CHILLI & COCONUT CREAM

For the salad, assemble:

50 g watercress
½ yellow pepper, sliced
100 g broccoli florets, chopped
2 spring onions, thinly sliced
½ red chilli, finely chopped
handful of fresh coriander leaves

For the dressing, mix:

1 tbsp extra virgin olive oil
1 tbsp Vegan Coconut dressing (page 26)
pinch of salt

CHICKEN, QUINOA, COURGETTE & CHERRY TOMATOES

For the salad, assemble:

½ courgette, shaved into ribbons with a vegetable peeler
50 g pre-cooked black and white quinoa
handful of cherry tomatoes, chopped
2 spring onions, chopped
50 g pre-roasted chicken, chopped
handful of pumpkin seeds
handful of fresh basil leaves

For the dressing, mix:

1 tbsp extra virgin olive oil
1 tsp balsamic vinegar
pinch salt and pepper

RAW

VEGAN
ALTERNATIVE
Add 50 g smoked tofu

CARROT, SUGAR SNAP PEAS & AVOCADO

For the salad, assemble:

50 g wild (or regular) rocket
handful of sugar snap peas or mangetout
½ carrot, cut into matchsticks
1 avocado, sliced
handful of pine nuts
3–4 edible violet flowers

For the dressing, blend together:

1 tbsp groundnut oil
pinch of salt
2 tbsp coconut milk
1 tbsp desiccated coconut
2 cm fresh ginger, peeled and grated

CANNELLINI BEANS & BABA GHANOUSH

For the salad, assemble:

*50 g mixed salad leaves (e.g. red oak leaf lettuce,
    watercress and rocket)*
100 g tinned cannellini beans
handful of sun-dried tomatoes, chopped
2 spring onions, thinly sliced
handful of pine nuts
3 tsp vegan baba ghanoush (aubergine dip)
handful of edible red and yellow nasturtium flowers

For the dressing, mix:

1 tbsp extra virgin olive oil
1 tsp balsamic vinegar
pinch of salt and pepper

OMNIVORE ALTERNATIVE

Replace the tuna with smoked ham or pastrami

TUNA, CHICKPEAS, GREEN BEANS & RED PEPPERS

For the salad, assemble:

1 red pepper, sliced
100 g steamed green beans
½ small red onion, thinly sliced
50 g tinned tuna (preserved in water), flaked
handful of tinned chickpeas
handful of fresh flat-leaf parsley leaves

For the dressing, mix:

1 tbsp extra virgin olive oil
1 tsp cider vinegar
pinch of salt and pepper

OMNIVORE

VEGETARIAN ALTERNATIVE
Replace the roasted beef with firm goats' cheese or brie, or even some Pecorino shavings

ROASTED BEEF, QUINOA, COURGETTE & MARINATED PEPPERS

For the salad, assemble:

1 courgette, shredded with a julienne peeler
50 g pre-cooked white quinoa
50 g roasted beef, thinly sliced
handful of marinated red peppers from a jar
handful of pumpkin seeds
handful of garlic sprouts

For the dressing, mix:

1 tbsp extra virgin olive oil
1 tsp balsamic vinegar
pinch of salt and pepper

VEGAN

VEGETARIAN ALTERNATIVE
Add 50 g Pecorino or Parmesan shavings

WHOLEWHEAT PASTA, CANNELLINI BEANS & TOMATOES

For the salad, assemble:

100 g pre-cooked wholewheat fusilli
100 g tinned cannellini beans
100 g cherry tomatoes, halved
handful of fresh basil leaves

For the dressing, mix:

1 tbsp chilli-infused extra virgin olive oil
1 tsp balsamic vinegar
pinch of salt and pepper

QUINOA, FETA, PEPPERS & BLACK OLIVES

For the salad, assemble:

100 g pre-cooked red and white quinoa
½ red pepper, diced
½ yellow pepper, diced
¼ red onion, diced
handful of pitted black olives, halved
50 g feta, cubed
handful of fresh flat-leaf parsley leaves

For the dressing, mix:

1 tbsp extra virgin olive oil
1 tsp balsamic vinegar
pinch of salt and pepper

RAW

VEGETARIAN ALTERNATIVE
Add 50 g cheese, such as goats' cheese or brie

BLACKBERRIES, MELON & HEMP SEEDS

For the salad, assemble:

50 g mixed salad leaves
100 g charentais or canteloupe melon, chopped
100 g blackberries
handful of shelled hemp seeds
4 edible violet flowers

For the dressing, mix:

1 tbsp extra virgin olive oil
1 tsp lemon juice
pinch of salt and pepper

VEGETARIAN

RAW
ALTERNATIVE
Replace the goats' cheese with pomegranate seeds, grapes or raisins

GOATS' CHEESE, MELON, BLUEBERRIES & SPINACH

For the salad, assemble:

50 g baby spinach
100 g charentais or canteloupe melon, chopped
handful of blueberries
50 g firm goats' cheese (or brie), chopped
1 tbsp shelled hemp seeds
handful of fresh mint leaves

For the dressing, mix:

1 tbsp extra virgin olive oil
1 tsp balsamic vinegar
pinch of salt and pepper

CHICKEN, QUINOA, SUN-DRIED TOMATOES & AVOCADO

For the salad, assemble:

50 g watercress
50 g cucumber, cut into long matchsticks
50 g pre-cooked red and white quinoa
½ avocado, chopped
handful of sun-dried tomatoes
50 g pre-roasted chicken, sliced
handful of fresh coriander leaves

For the dressing, mix:

1 tbsp extra virgin olive oil
1 tsp balsamic vinegar
pinch of salt and pepper

GOATS' CHEESE, KALE, CUCUMBER & TOMATOES

For the salad, assemble:

50 g kale, finely chopped (discard the stems)
100 g cucumber, cut into long matchsticks
100 g tomatoes, chopped
50 g firm goats' cheese (or brie), chopped
handful of pine nuts
handful of fresh basil leaves

For the dressing, mix:

1 tbsp extra virgin olive oil
1 tsp balsamic vinegar
pinch of salt and pepper

PESCATARIAN

VEGAN
ALTERNATIVE
*Replace the roasted
salmon with 1 tbsp
sesame seeds or linseeds*

SALMON, BLACK BEANS & WHOLEWHEAT PASTA

For the salad, assemble:

100 g pre-cooked wholewheat penne
100 g tinned black beans
100 g cherry tomatoes
*50 g raw or pre-steamed broccoli florets,
    chopped*
50 g roasted salmon, flaked
2 spring onions, chopped
1 tsp nori (toasted seaweed) sprinkle

For the dressing, mix:

1 tbsp extra virgin olive oil
1 tsp cider vinegar
pinch of salt and pepper

VEGAN

VEGETARIAN
ALTERNATIVE
*Add 50 g Pecorino or
Parmesan shavings*

BARLEY & ROASTED AUBERGINE & RED ONION

For the salad, assemble:

100 g pre-cooked barley
1 finely chopped and pre-roasted aubergine
1 sliced and pre-roasted red onion
handful of fresh basil leaves

For the dressing, mix:

1 tbsp extra virgin olive oil
1 tsp balsamic vinegar
pinch of salt and pepper

SMOKED HAM, FETA, CABBAGE & CHERRY TOMATOES

For the salad, assemble:

100 g pointed/sweetheart cabbage, shredded
100 g cherry tomatoes, quartered
50 g cucumber, chopped
50 g feta, cubed
50 g smoked ham, sliced
bunch of fresh chives, snipped
a few fresh flat-leaf parsley leaves

For the dressing, mix:

1 tbsp extra virgin olive oil
1 tsp cider vinegar
pinch of salt and pepper

RAW

VEGAN ALTERNATIVE
Add 100 g edamame beans, or tinned black-eyed peas or chickpeas

CAVOLO NERO, RED PEPPER & CUCUMBER

For the salad, assemble:

2–3 leaves of cavolo nero, shredded (discard the stems)
100 g cucumber, cut into matchsticks
½ small red romano pepper, sliced
handful of pine nuts
handful of fresh coriander leaves

For the dressing, mix:

2 tsp sweet white miso (or soya cream)
1 tbsp groundnut oil
1 tsp cider vinegar
pinch of salt and pepper
1 tsp agave nectar
2 cm fresh ginger, peeled and grated

VEGAN

VEGETARIAN ALTERNATIVE

Replace the oat cream with natural yoghurt or double cream

QUINOA, CHICKPEAS & ROASTED AUBERGINE

For the salad, assemble:

150 g pre-cooked red and white quinoa
100 g tinned chickpeas
½ chopped and pre-roasted aubergine
handful of fresh flat-leaf parsley leaves

For the dressing, mix:

1 tbsp extra virgin olive oil
1 tsp cider vinegar
pinch of salt
1 tsp tahini
1 tbsp oat cream
2 pinches of saffron threads

VEGAN
ALTERNATIVE
*Replace the tuna
with celery*

TUNA, CHICKPEAS & CHERRY TOMATOES

For the salad, assemble:

100 g cherry tomatoes, quartered
100 g tinned chickpeas
½ little gem lettuce
100 g tinned tuna (preserved in water), flaked
bunch of fresh chives, snipped

For the dressing, mix:

1 tbsp extra virgin olive oil
1 tsp lemon juice
pinch of salt and pepper

AUTUMN

VEGAN

OMNIVORE
ALTERNATIVE
*Add 50 g roasted
chicken breast
or chorizo*

BLACK BEANS, AVOCADO & BROWN RICE

For the salad, assemble:

100 g cooked brown basmati rice
100 g tinned black beans
½ avocado, chopped
handful of cherry tomatoes, quartered
handful of fresh coriander leaves
1 small red chilli, finely chopped

For the dressing, mix:

1 tbsp extra virgin olive oil
1 tsp lemon juice
pinch of salt and pepper

OAK-SMOKED CHEDDAR, PLUMS & RASPBERRIES

For the salad, assemble:

50 g baby spinach
2 yellow plums, chopped
100 g raspberries
50 g oak-smoked Cheddar, chopped
handful of pine nuts
handful of fresh mint leaves

For the dressing, mix:

1 tbsp extra virgin olive oil
1 tsp balsamic vinegar
pinch of salt and pepper

PESCATARIAN

RAW ALTERNATIVE

Replace the hot-smoked salmon with 1 avocado and ½ small red chilli, and use freshly shucked corn

HOT-SMOKED SALMON, CORN & BROCCOLI

For the salad, assemble:

50 g rocket
100 g fresh or tinned sweetcorn
100 g broccoli florets, chopped
50 g hot-smoked salmon, flaked
bunch of fresh chives, snipped

For the dressing, mix:

1 tbsp extra virgin olive oil
1 tsp balsamic vinegar
pinch of salt and pepper

OMNIVORE

VEGETARIAN ALTERNATIVE
Replace the ham with mozzarella cheese or ricotta

SMOKED HAM, COUSCOUS, BROCCOLI & PEAS

For the salad, assemble:

100 g pre-cooked wholewheat couscous
50 g pre-steamed peas
100 g broccoli florets, chopped
50 g smoked ham, sliced
bunch of fresh chives, trimmed

For the dressing, mix:

1 tbsp extra virgin olive oil
1 tsp cider vinegar
pinch of salt and pepper
pinch of dried parsley

PESCATARIAN
ALTERNATIVE
*Add 50 g cooked fish
or seafood, such as tuna,
sardines, anchovies,
salmon or prawns*

BROCCOLI, CORN & CHERRY TOMATOES

For the salad, assemble:

60 g red oak leaf lettuce
50 g cherry tomatoes, halved
100 g broccoli florets, chopped
handful of freshly shucked sweetcorn
handful of fresh flat-leaf parsley leaves
2 spring onions, chopped

For the dressing, mix:

1 tbsp extra virgin olive oil
1 tsp cider vinegar
pinch of salt and pepper

CANNELLINI BEANS, TOMATOES & HOUMOUS

For the salad, assemble:

50 g mixed salad leaves
150 g cherry tomatoes, halved
150 g tinned cannellini beans

For the dressing, mix:

1 tbsp extra virgin olive oil
1 tsp cider vinegar
1 tbsp vegan houmous
pinch of salt and pepper

OMNIVORE

RAW ALTERNATIVE
Replace the chicken with mangetout or sugar snap peas, and the quinoa with baby corn

ROASTED CHICKEN, QUINOA, RED PEPPER & PEANUTS

For the salad, assemble:

100 g pre-cooked red and white quinoa
½ small red romano pepper, sliced
handful of bean sprouts
50 g pre-roasted chicken, sliced
handful of peanuts
2 spring onions, thinly sliced
handful of fresh coriander leaves

For the dressing, mix:

1 tbsp vegetable oil
1 tsp lime juice
pinch of salt
pinch of chilli powder
1 tsp agave nectar

PESCATARIAN

VEGAN
ALTERNATIVE
*Replace the mackerel
with cucumber and add
a further 50 g quinoa*

SMOKED MACKEREL, QUINOA & COURGETTE

For the salad, assemble:

*1 small courgette, shaved into ribbons with
  a vegetable peeler
100 g red and yellow cherry tomatoes, halved
50 g pre-cooked black quinoa
50 g smoked mackerel, flaked
handful of fresh flat-leaf parsley leaves*

For the dressing, mix:

*1 tbsp extra virgin olive oil
1 tsp lemon juice
pinch of salt and pepper*

SHIITAKE MUSHROOMS, RED PEPPER & NORI

For the salad, assemble:

50 g rocket
½ red pepper, sliced
100 g sliced and pre-fried shiitake mushrooms
*handful of shredded and pre-toasted nori (toasted
   seaweed), tossed with a dash of sunflower oil and
   soy sauce*
1 tsp toasted sesame seeds
2 spring onions, thinly sliced

For the dressing, mix:

1 tbsp vegetable oil
1 tsp toasted sesame oil
1 tsp tamari soy sauce
pinch of salt and pepper

TUNA, COURGETTE, BROCCOLI & BLACK OLIVES

For the salad, assemble:

50 g baby spinach
½ courgette, shaved into ribbons with a vegetable peeler
50 g broccoli florets, chopped
50 g tinned tuna (preserved in water), flaked
handful of pitted black olives
bunch of fresh chives, trimmed

For the dressing, mix:

1 tbsp extra virgin olive oil
1 tsp cider vinegar
pinch of salt and pepper

RAW

OMNIVORE
ALTERNATIVE
*Add 50 g roasted beef
or smoked ham*

BROCCOLI, CARROT & CHERRY TOMATOES

For the salad, assemble:

*1 purple (or regular) carrot, shaved into ribbons with
  a vegetable peeler*
100 g broccoli florets, chopped
100 g cherry tomatoes, quartered
handful of capers
2 tbsp pumpkin seeds
2 tbsp shelled hemp seeds

For the dressing, mix:

1 tbsp extra virgin olive oil
1 tsp cider vinegar
pinch of salt and pepper

GREEN BEANS, NEW POTATOES & BROCCOLI

For the salad, assemble:

4–5 halved pre-steamed new potatoes
50 g pre-steamed green beans
50 g pre-steamed broccoli florets
handful of pine nuts
sprinkle of fresh thyme leaves

For the dressing, mix:

1 tbsp extra virgin olive oil
1 tsp cider vinegar
1 tbsp vegan cream (e.g. soya or oat)
pinch of salt and pepper

VEGETARIAN

VEGAN
ALTERNATIVE
*Replace the blue cheese
with 100 g steamed
beans, such as edamame
or broad beans*

FENNEL, BLUE CHEESE & PISTACHIOS

For the salad, assemble:

60 g romaine lettuce, torn
½ fennel, thinly sliced
50 g blue cheese, crumbled
handful of toasted pistachios

For the dressing, mix:

1 tbsp extra virgin olive oil
1 tsp balsamic vinegar
pinch of salt and pepper
1 tbsp fennel seeds

VEGETARIAN

RAW ALTERNATIVE

Replace the feta with a further handful of almonds and raisins

FETA, RED PEPPER, CELERY & ALMONDS

For the salad, assemble:

2 celery stalks, sliced
1 red pepper, sliced
50 g feta, cubed
handful of almonds, chopped
handful of raisins
pinch of chilli flakes

For the dressing, mix:

1 tbsp extra virgin olive oil
1 tsp balsamic vinegar
pinch of salt and pepper

VEGAN

PESCATARIAN ALTERNATIVE
Add some roasted salmon or cooked prawns

QUINOA, FRIED COURGETTE & ROCKET

For the salad, assemble:

50 g rocket
100 g pre-cooked red and white quinoa
1 chopped and pre-fried courgette
bunch of fresh basil leaves

For the dressing, mix:

1 tbsp extra virgin olive oil
1 tsp balsamic vinegar
pinch of salt and pepper

QUINOA, SUGAR SNAP PEAS, BROCCOLI & MUSHROOMS

For the salad, assemble:

*100 g pre-cooked red and white quinoa
handful of sugar snap peas
100 g broccoli florets, chopped
50 g button mushrooms, sliced
50 g Parmesan shavings
handful of walnuts, chopped
handful of fresh flat-leaf parsley leaves*

For the dressing, mix:

*1 tbsp extra virgin olive oil
1 tsp balsamic vinegar
pinch of salt and pepper*

OMNIVORE

VEGETARIAN ALTERNATIVE

Replace the beef with 100 g tinned chickpeas or white beans

ROASTED BEEF, CARROT & BABY CHARD

For the salad, assemble:

50 g baby chard
1 carrot, shredded with a julienne peeler
50 g pre-roasted beef, thinly sliced
50 g Pecorino shavings
handful of fresh chives, trimmed

For the dressing, mix:

1 tbsp extra virgin olive oil
1 tsp balsamic vinegar
pinch of salt and pepper

PESCATARIAN

VEGAN ALTERNATIVE
Replace the prawns with a handful of edamame beans

PRAWNS, RED RICE, CUCUMBER & NORI

For the salad, assemble:

100 g cucumber, cut into long thin matchsticks
80 g pre-cooked red rice
50 g pre-cooked prawns
2 spring onions, sliced
1 tsp nori (toasted seaweed) sprinkle
1 tsp poppy seeds

For the dressing, mix:

1 tbsp extra virgin olive oil
1 tsp light soy sauce
1 tsp wasabi powder
1 tsp ground ginger
1 tsp toasted sesame oil

CAVOLO NERO, RASPBERRIES & BLACKBERRIES

For the salad, assemble:

100 g cavolo nero, shredded (discard the stems)
handful of raspberries
handful of blackberries

For the dressing, blend together:

1 tbsp extra virgin olive oil
handful of almonds, pre-soaked in water overnight
*   then drained*
1 tbsp water
1 tsp lemon juice
pinch of salt

ROASTED AUBERGINE, CHICKPEAS & POMEGRANATE

For the salad, assemble:

1 small cucumber, cut into long thin matchsticks
100 g tinned chickpeas
handful of pomegranate seeds
1 cubed and pre-roasted aubergine
handful of fresh mint leaves

For the dressing, mix:

1 tbsp extra virgin olive oil
2 tbsp soya cream
pinch of salt and pepper

OMNIVORE

RAW
ALTERNATIVE
*Replace the coppa ham
with the other half of
the pear*

COPPA HAM, PEAR, BLACKBERRIES & WALNUTS

For the salad, assemble:

50 g mixed salad leaves
handful of blackberries
½ pear, chopped
handful of pomegranate seeds
50 g coppa ham, thinly sliced
handful of walnuts

For the dressing, mix:

1 tbsp extra virgin olive oil
1 tsp balsamic vinegar
pinch of salt and pepper

BLACKBERRIES, COTTAGE CHEESE, SPINACH & CROUTONS

For the salad, assemble:

50 g baby spinach
100 g blackberries
handful of wholewheat croutons
100 g cottage cheese
bunch of fresh chives, snipped

For the dressing, mix:

1 tbsp extra virgin olive oil
1 tsp balsamic vinegar
pinch of salt and pepper

VEGAN

OMNIVORE
ALTERNATIVE
*Add 50 g roasted
chicken*

ROASTED AUBERGINE, TOMATOES & PESTO

For the salad, assemble:

60 g red oak leaf lettuce (or mixed salad leaves)
100 g tomatoes, chopped
1 cubed and pre-roasted aubergine
handful of fresh basil leaves

For the dressing, mix:

1 tbsp extra virgin olive oil
1 tbsp Raw Green Pesto (page 25)
pinch of salt and pepper

RAW

VEGETARIAN ALTERNATIVE
Add 50 g firm goats' cheese, brie or blue cheese, such as stilton

CARROT, MUSHROOMS, POMEGRANATE & WALNUTS

For the salad, assemble:

60 g mixed salad leaves
1 purple (or regular) carrot, shaved into ribbons
* with a vegetable peeler*
100 g brown mushrooms, sliced
handful of pomegranate seeds
handful of walnuts, chopped
handful of fresh flat-leaf parsley leaves

For the dressing, mix:

1 tbsp extra virgin olive oil
1 tsp cider vinegar
pinch of salt and pepper
2 tbsp Nut & Lemon dressing
* (page 26, made with walnuts)*

RAW

PESCATARIAN ALTERNATIVE
Add 50 g cooked prawns

RED PEPPER, CARROT & CASHEW NUTS

For the salad, assemble:

1 carrot, shaved into ribbons with a vegetable peeler
1 red romano pepper, sliced
2 spring onions, thinly sliced
handful of cashew nuts
handful of fresh coriander leaves

For the dressing, blend together:

2 tbsp coconut water
2 tbsp cashew nuts
1 tbsp vegetable oil
1 tsp lemon juice
1 tsp ground ginger

RAW ALTERNATIVE
Replace the feta with pumpkin seeds, and use raw olives

FETA, YELLOW PEPPER, SPINACH & BLACK OLIVES

For the salad, assemble:

50 g baby spinach
1 yellow pepper, sliced
½ small red onion, thinly sliced
50 g feta, cubed
handful of pitted black olives, halved

For the dressing, mix:

1 tbsp extra virgin olive oil
1 tsp cider vinegar
pinch of salt and pepper

PESCATARIAN

VEGETARIAN ALTERNATIVE
Replace the anchovies with goats' cheese or feta

ANCHOVIES, CAULIFLOWER, CAPERS & TOMATOES

For the salad, assemble:

100 g cauliflower florets, finely chopped
60 g cherry tomatoes, chopped
handful of capers
50 g marinated anchovies, chopped
handful of fresh flat-leaf parsley leaves
bunch of fresh chives, trimmed

For the dressing, mix:

1 tbsp extra virgin olive oil
1 tsp balsamic vinegar
pinch of salt
pinch of red pepper

VEGETARIAN

VEGAN ALTERNATIVE

Replace the feta with
100 g tinned white beans,
such as cannellini or
haricot

FETA, COUSCOUS & ROASTED AUBERGINE

For the salad, assemble:

100 g cooked wholewheat couscous
½ cubed and pre-roasted aubergine
handful of sun-dried tomatoes
50 g feta, cubed
handful of fresh mint leaves

For the dressing, mix:

1 tbsp extra virgin olive oil
1 tsp balsamic vinegar
pinch of salt and pepper

RAW

VEGAN ALTERNATIVE
Add 100 g tinned chickpeas or steamed green beans

BEETROOT, COURGETTE, POMEGRANATE & ALFALFA

For the salad, assemble:

50 g mixed salad leaves (e.g. watercress, rocket, chard and red oak leaf lettuce)
1 small beetroot, diced
1 courgette, cut into matchsticks
handful of pomegranate seeds
1 tbsp shelled hemp seeds
handful of alfalfa sprouts

For the dressing, mix:

1 tbsp extra virgin olive oil
1 tsp cider vinegar
pinch of salt and pepper
1 tbsp raw mustard (made from soaking 2 tbsp yellow mustard seeds, 2 tbsp brown mustard seeds, 2 tbsp cider vinegar, 1 tbsp water and 1 tsp agave nectar together overnight then blending them)

ROASTED BEEF, BEETROOT, POMEGRANATE & ORANGE ZEST

For the salad, assemble:

50 g baby spinach
½ beetroot, thinly sliced
handful of pomegranate seeds
100 g pre-roasted beef, thinly sliced
sprinkle of pared orange zest
handful of walnuts, chopped
sprinkle of fresh thyme leaves

For the dressing, mix:

1 tbsp extra virgin olive oil
1 tsp orange juice
pinch of salt and pepper

VEGETARIAN

VEGAN
ALTERNATIVE
*Replace the Pecorino
with cashew nuts
or pine nuts*

PECORINO, SUN-DRIED TOMATOES & GREEN BEANS

For the salad, assemble:

100 g pre-steamed green beans
handful of sun-dried tomatoes, sliced
50 g Pecorino shavings
2 spring onions, thinly sliced
handful of fresh flat-leaf parsley leaves

For the dressing, mix:

1 tbsp extra virgin olive oil
1 tsp balsamic vinegar
pinch of salt and pepper

TUNA, COUSCOUS, GREEN BEANS & CHERRY TOMATOES

For the salad, assemble:

100 g cooked couscous
100 g pre-steamed green beans
100 g cherry tomatoes, halved
50 g tinned tuna (preserved in water), flaked
handful of fresh flat-leaf parsley leaves

For the dressing, mix:

1 tbsp extra virgin olive oil
1 tsp lemon juice
pinch of salt and pepper

VEGAN

PESCATARIAN
ALTERNATIVE
*Add some marinated
anchovies or smoked
mackerel*

BUTTER BEANS, COURGETTE & BLACK OLIVES

For the salad, assemble:

1 little gem lettuce
1 courgette, shredded with a julienne peeler
100 g tinned butter beans
handful of fresh basil leaves
handful of pitted black olives, halved

For the dressing, mix:

1 tsp extra virgin olive oil
1 tbsp Olive Tapenade (page 25)
1 tsp cider vinegar
pinch of salt and pepper

RAW

VEGAN
ALTERNATIVE
*Add 50 g steamed green
beans or peas, or some
cooked red quinoa*

SUN-DRIED TOMATOES, COURGETTE & PINE NUTS

For the salad, assemble:

*2 small courgettes, shaved into ribbons with
    a vegetable peeler*
handful of sun-dried tomatoes
handful of raw pitted black olives, halved
handful of pine nuts
handful of fresh dill fronds

For the dressing, mix:

1 tbsp extra virgin olive oil
1 tsp cider vinegar
pinch of salt and pepper

RAW

VEGETARIAN ALTERNATIVE
Add some medium-hard cheese, such as Manchego, gouda or Cheddar

CAVOLO NERO, AVOCADO & SPROUTED BEANS

For the salad, assemble:

100 g cavolo nero, shredded (discard the stems)
100 g cherry tomatoes, halved
¼ small red onion, finely chopped
1 avocado, chopped
handful of sprouted beans

For the dressing, mix:

1 tbsp extra virgin olive oil
1 tsp cider vinegar
pinch of salt and pepper

TUNA, CAVOLO NERO, CARROT & SUN-DRIED TOMATOES

For the salad, assemble:

50 g cavolo nero, shredded (discard the stems)
*½ small carrot, shaved into ribbons with
 a vegetable peeler*
handful of sun-dried tomatoes
50 g tinned tuna (preserved in water), flaked
handful of pine nuts
bunch of fresh chives, snipped

For the dressing, mix:

1 tbsp extra virgin olive oil
1 tsp lemon juice
pinch of salt and pepper

OMNIVORE

VEGETARIAN ALTERNATIVE

Replace the speck with more celery and blue cheese

SPECK, BLUE CHEESE, BLACKBERRIES & CELERY

For the salad, assemble:

50 g mixed salad leaves
handful of blackberries
1 celery stalk, sliced
50 g speck ham, thinly sliced
50 g blue cheese, crumbled
handful of walnuts, chopped
handful of fresh mint leaves

For the dressing, mix:

1 tbsp extra virgin olive oil
1 tsp balsamic vinegar
pinch of salt and pepper

RAW

VEGETARIAN ALTERNATIVE
Add cheese, such as salted ricotta, goats' cheese or young Pecorino

FIGS, BLACKBERRIES & HAZELNUTS

For the salad, assemble:

50 g mixed salad leaves (e.g. chard, watercress and red oak leaf lettuce)
handful of blackberries
2 figs, cut into wedges
handful of hazelnuts, chopped
handful of fresh mint leaves

For the dressing, mix:

1 tbsp extra virgin olive oil
1 tsp cider vinegar
pinch of salt and pepper

RAW ALTERNATIVE
Replace the Pecorino with a handful of raspberries or cherries, or a peach

PECORINO, BLACK GRAPES & PINE NUTS

For the salad, assemble:

100 g mixed baby salad leaves (e.g. watercress, chard and red oak leaf lettuce)
100 g black grapes, halved
50 g Pecorino shavings
handful of pine nuts

For the dressing, mix:

1 tbsp extra virgin olive oil
1 tsp balsamic vinegar
pinch of salt and pepper

RAW

VEGETARIAN
ALTERNATIVE
Replace the Nut &
Lemon dressing with
single cream or
natural yoghurt

RED GRAPES, CELERY & WALNUTS

For the salad, assemble:

50 g rocket
handful of red grapes, halved
2 celery stalks, sliced
handful of walnuts, chopped
handful of fresh flat-leaf parsley leaves

For the dressing, mix:

1 tbsp extra virgin olive oil
1 tsp lemon juice
pinch of salt and pepper
2 tbsp Nut & Lemon dressing
  (page 26, made with walnuts)

PESCATARIAN

VEGETARIAN ALTERNATIVE

Replace the prawns with a mild cheese, such as Cheddar or Manchego

PRAWNS, COURGETTE, CARROT & PINE NUTS

For the salad, assemble:

½ small courgette, shaved into ribbons with a vegetable peeler

½ small purple (or regular) carrot, shaved into ribbons with a vegetable peeler

30 g rocket

50 g pre-cooked prawns

handful of pine nuts

bunch of fresh chives, snipped

For the dressing, mix:

1 tbsp extra virgin olive oil

1 tbsp mayonnaise

1 tsp cider vinegar

pinch of salt and pepper

1 tsp smoked paprika

CANNELLINI BEANS, COURGETTE & PESTO

For the salad, assemble:

1 courgette, shredded with a julienne peeler
100 g tinned cannellini beans
2 spring onions, thinly sliced
handful of pine nuts
handful of fresh basil leaves

For the dressing, mix:

1 tbsp extra virgin olive oil
1 tsp balsamic vinegar
pinch of salt and pepper
2 tbsp Raw Green Pesto (page 25)

VEGETARIAN ALTERNATIVE
Replace the chicken with tinned cannellini beans or lentils

ROASTED CHICKEN & COURGETTE, CABBAGE & MANCHEGO

For the salad, assemble:

100 g green or savoy cabbage, finely shredded
1 cubed and pre-roasted courgette
50 g pre-roasted chicken, sliced
50 g Manchego (or gouda or Cheddar), cubed
handful of fresh lemon thyme leaves

For the dressing, mix:

1 tbsp extra virgin olive oil
1 tsp balsamic vinegar
pinch of salt and pepper

GOUDA, BLACK BEANS, CORN & SUN-DRIED TOMATOES

For the salad, assemble:

50 g salad leaves (e.g. frisée and lamb's lettuce)
100 g tinned black beans
handful of fresh or tinned sweetcorn
handful of sun-dried tomatoes, sliced
50 g gouda (or Manchego or Cheddar), cubed
handful of fresh coriander leaves

For the dressing, mix:

1 tbsp chilli-infused extra virgin olive oil
1 tsp balsamic vinegar
pinch of salt and pepper

VEGAN ALTERNATIVE

Replace the anchovies with a handful of capers and a handful of black olives

ANCHOVIES, COUSCOUS, CUCUMBER & LEMON ZEST

For the salad, assemble:

100 g pre-cooked giant Palestinian couscous
100 g cucumber, chopped
50 g marinated anchovies, chopped
sprinkle of pared lemon zest
handful of fresh flat-leaf parsley leaves

For the dressing, mix:

1 tbsp extra virgin olive oil
1 tsp lemon juice
pinch of salt and pepper
pinch of chilli flakes

VEGAN

OMNIVORE
ALTERNATIVE
*Add 50 g roasted
chicken breast*

GLUTEN-FREE PASTA, BLACK OLIVES & CHILLI

For the salad, assemble:

100 g pre-cooked gluten-free penne
100 g cherry tomatoes, halved
2 spring onions, thinly sliced
handful of pitted black olives, chopped
handful of fresh flat-leaf parsley leaves
1 small red chilli, deseeded and thinly sliced

For the dressing, mix:

1 tbsp extra virgin olive oil
pinch of salt and pepper

OMNIVORE
ALTERNATIVE
*Add 50 g roasted beef
or smoked ham*

RED CABBAGE, YELLOW TOMATOES & RED PEPPER

For the salad, assemble:

100 g red cabbage, finely shredded
1 red pepper, thinly sliced
100 g yellow tomatoes, chopped
1 tsp pumpkin seeds
sprinkle of fresh thyme leaves

For the dressing, mix:

1 tbsp extra virgin olive oil
1 tsp cider vinegar
pinch of salt and pepper

PARMA HAM, MANGO, TARRAGON & SESAME SEEDS

For the salad, assemble:

80 g mixed salad leaves (e.g. watercress and wild rocket)
100 g mango, sliced
2 spring onions, thinly sliced
50 g Parma ham, thinly sliced
1 tbsp sesame seeds
handful of fresh tarragon leaves

For the dressing, mix:

1 tbsp extra virgin olive oil
1 tsp balsamic vinegar
pinch of salt and pepper

SCAMORZA, SPELT, ARTICHOKES & CARROT

For the salad, assemble:

100 g pre-cooked spelt
*1 small carrot, shaved into ribbons with a
vegetable peeler*
*handful of grilled, marinated artichoke hearts,
chopped*
50 g scamorza (smoked cheese), cubed
1 tbsp sesame seeds
handful of fresh flat-leaf parsley leaves

For the dressing, mix:

1 tbsp extra virgin olive oil
1 tsp balsamic vinegar
pinch of salt and pepper

SMOKED MACKEREL, COUSCOUS & ROASTED BEETROOT

For the salad, assemble:

100 g cooked wholewheat couscous
1 roasted beetroot, chopped
50 g broccoli florets, chopped
50 g smoked mackerel, flaked
1 tbsp mustard seeds
handful of fresh flat-leaf parsley leaves

For the dressing, mix:

1 tbsp extra virgin olive oil
1 tsp lemon juice
pinch of salt and pepper

BRESAOLA, QUINOA, CORN & BROCCOLI

For the salad, assemble:

100 g pre-cooked white quinoa
50 g broccoli florets, chopped
50 g cherry tomatoes, halved
50 g fresh or tinned sweetcorn
1 spring onion, thinly sliced
50 g bresaola (air-dried beef), thinly sliced
handful of fresh flat-leaf parsley leaves

For the dressing, mix:

1 tbsp extra virgin olive oil
1 tsp cider vinegar
pinch of salt and pepper

VEGAN

VEGETARIAN ALTERNATIVE
Add some shavings of a mature cheese, such as Pecorino, Parmesan or aged Cheddar

FENNEL, BROCCOLI, POMEGRANATE & HOUMOUS

For the salad, assemble:

50 g rocket
50 g broccoli florets, chopped
½ small fennel bulb, thinly sliced
handful of pomegranate seeds
2 spring onions, sliced
1 tbsp sesame seeds
handful of fresh mint leaves

For the dressing, mix:

1 tbsp extra virgin olive oil
1 tsp cider vinegar
1 tbsp vegan houmous
pinch of salt and pepper
pinch of smoked paprika

RAW

VEGETARIAN ALTERNATIVE

Replace the Nut & Lemon dressing with natural yoghurt

FIGS, FENNEL & POMEGRANATE

For the salad, assemble:

50 g rocket
1 small fennel bulb, thinly sliced
2 figs, quartered
handful of pomegranate seeds
bunch of fresh chives, trimmed

For the dressing, mix:

1 tbsp extra virgin olive oil
1 tsp lemon juice
pinch of salt and pepper
2 tbsp Nut & Lemon dressing
(page 26, made with cashew nuts)

VEGETARIAN

RAW
ALTERNATIVE
Replace the goats'
cheese with a handful of
blueberries or red grapes

FIGS, GOATS' CHEESE & WALNUTS

For the salad, assemble:

50 g baby spinach
2 figs, quartered
50 g firm goats' cheese, chopped
handful of walnuts
handful of fresh mint leaves

For the dressing, mix:

1 tbsp extra virgin olive oil
1 tsp balsamic vinegar
pinch of salt and pepper

RAW

OMNIVORE
ALTERNATIVE
*Add 50 g roasted beef
or ham, and replace the
Raw Nut & Agave
dressing with mayo*

KALE, GREEN BEANS & CHERRY TOMATOES

For the salad, assemble:

70 g kale, finely chopped (discard the stems)
handful of cherry tomatoes, chopped
handful of green beans or sugar snap peas
1 tbsp sesame seeds
handful of fresh mint leaves

For the dressing, mix:

1 tbsp extra virgin olive oil
1 tsp cider vinegar
2 tbsp Raw Nut & Agave dressing (page 27,
   made with sesame seeds instead of cashew nuts)
pinch of salt and pepper

SMOKED MACKEREL, BROCCOLI & CHERRY TOMATOES

For the salad, assemble:

50 g watercress
100 g broccoli florets, chopped
handful of yellow and red cherry tomatoes, halved
50 g smoked mackerel, flaked
handful of pine nuts
handful of fresh flat-leaf parsley leaves

For the dressing, mix:

1 tbsp extra virgin olive oil
1 tsp lemon juice
pinch of salt and pepper

VEGETARIAN

PESCATARIAN
ALTERNATIVE
*Replace the Parmesan
with smoked salmon*

QUAIL EGGS, PARMESAN, FENNEL & SUN-DRIED TOMATOES

For the salad, assemble:

50 g rocket
½ fennel bulb, thinly sliced
handful of sun-dried tomatoes, chopped
3–4 hard-boiled quail eggs, halved
50 g Parmesan shavings
handful of pine nuts
handful of fresh flat-leaf parsley leaves

For the dressing, mix:

1 tbsp extra virgin olive oil
1 tsp cider vinegar
pinch of salt and pepper

PURPLE POTATOES, PEAS & CARROT

For the salad, assemble:

*1 carrot, shaved into ribbons with a
   vegetable peeler*
50 g fresh or pre-steamed peas
*100 g chopped and pre-steamed purple
   (or regular) new potatoes*
handful of fresh flat-leaf parsley leaves

For the dressing, mix:

1 tsp extra virgin olive oil
1 tbsp vegan cream (e.g. oat or soya)
1 tsp cider vinegar
pinch of salt
pinch of saffron threads

OMNIVORE

VEGAN
ALTERNATIVE
Replace the chicken with 100 g of your favourite tinned beans

ROASTED CHICKEN, BLACK QUINOA & MARINATED PEPPERS

For the salad, assemble:

50 g rocket
50 g pre-cooked black quinoa
handful of marinated peppers from a jar
50 g pre-roasted chicken, sliced
handful of fresh coriander leaves

For the dressing, mix:

1 tbsp extra virgin olive oil
1 tsp balsamic vinegar
pinch of salt and pepper

VEGAN

VEGETARIAN ALTERNATIVE
Add 50 g Pecorino

ROASTED VEG, GIANT COUSCOUS & BLACK OLIVES

For the salad, assemble:

100 g pre-cooked giant Palestinian couscous
½ yellow pepper, ½ red pepper, 1 small courgette
  and 1 small red onion — all cubed and pre-roasted
50 g rocket
handful of pitted black olives, halved

For the dressing, mix:

1 tbsp extra virgin olive oil
1 tsp balsamic vinegar
pinch of salt and pepper

SQUID, BROCCOLI & AVOCADO

For the salad, assemble:

50 g watercress
50 g broccoli florets, chopped
1 avocado, chopped
50 g pre-grilled squid, sliced
handful of pumpkin seeds
bunch of fresh chives, snipped

For the dressing, mix:

1 tbsp extra virgin olive oil
1 tsp lemon juice
pinch of salt and pepper
pinch of chilli flakes

PASTRAMI, BROWN RICE & ROASTED COURGETTE

For the salad, assemble:

50 g pre-cooked brown short-grain rice
100 g cucumber, shredded with a julienne peeler
(discard the soft core)
1 small cubed and pre-roasted courgette
50 g pastrami or roasted beef, thinly sliced
handful of fresh mint leaves

For the dressing, mix:

1 tbsp extra virgin olive oil
1 tsp balsamic vinegar
pinch of salt and pepper

OMNIVORE

PESCATARIAN
ALTERNATIVE
*Replace the chicken with
tinned tuna or smoked
mackerel*

ROASTED CHICKEN, SPELT & BROCCOLI

For the salad, assemble:

100 g pre-cooked spelt
100 g raw or pre-steamed broccoli florets, chopped
100 g cherry tomatoes, chopped
50 g pre-roasted chicken, sliced
2 spring onions, thinly sliced
handful of fresh flat-leaf parsley leaves

For the dressing, mix:

1 tbsp extra virgin olive oil
1 tsp balsamic vinegar
pinch of salt and pepper

VEGAN

VEGETARIAN ALTERNATIVE
Add 50 g goats' cheese or blue cheese

ARTICHOKES, BUTTER BEANS, CELERY & WALNUTS

For the salad, assemble:

2 celery stalks, sliced
100 g tinned butter beans
handful of grilled, marinated artichoke hearts, chopped
handful of walnuts, chopped
bunch of fresh chives, snipped

For the dressing, mix:

1 tbsp extra virgin olive oil
1 tsp balsamic vinegar
pinch of salt and pepper

WINTER

SPECK, SCAMORZA, SUN-DRIED TOMATOES & RADICCHIO

For the salad, assemble:

70 g radicchio
50 g scamorza (smoked cheese), finely chopped
50 g speck ham, roughly shredded
handful of sun-dried tomatoes, chopped

For the dressing, mix:

1 tbsp extra virgin olive oil
1 tsp balsamic vinegar
pinch of salt and pepper

MANCHEGO, DRIED APRICOTS, FENNEL & RADICCHIO

For the salad, assemble:

100 g radicchio, shredded
½ fennel bulb, thinly sliced
handful of unsulphured dried apricots, chopped
50 g Manchego (or Asiago or gouda), cubed
handful of almonds
handful of fresh mint leaves

For the dressing, mix:

1 tbsp extra virgin olive oil
1 tsp cider vinegar
pinch of salt and pepper

PESCATARIAN

VEGAN
ALTERNATIVE
Replace the salmon and caviar with 100 g tinned chickpeas, seasoned with a pinch of paprika

SASHIMI SALMON, CAVIAR, PARSNIP & RADICCHIO

For the salad, assemble:

50 g radicchio, shredded

1 small parsnip, shaved into ribbons with a vegetable peeler

50 g sashimi salmon, thinly sliced

1 tsp lumpfish caviar

1 tsp toasted sesame seeds

bunch of fresh chives, snipped

For the dressing, mix:

1 tbsp extra virgin olive oil

1 tsp lemon juice

pinch of salt

VEGAN

BLACK LENTILS, PARSNIPS & DRIED CRANBERRIES

For the salad, assemble:

100 g pre-cooked black lentils
2 parsnips, shaved into ribbons with
*   a vegetable peeler*
handful of dried cranberries
handful of pine nuts
bunch of fresh chives, snipped

For the dressing, mix:

1 tbsp extra virgin olive oil
1 tsp balsamic vinegar
pinch of salt and pepper

RAW

VEGETARIAN
ALTERNATIVE
*Add 50 g goats' or blue
cheese, or Pecorino*

PEAR, CAULIFLOWER, KALE & PISTACHIOS

For the salad, assemble:

70 g kale (discard the stems), chopped
1 pear, chopped
100 g cauliflower florets, chopped
bunch of fresh chives, snipped
handful of pistachios

For the dressing, mix:

1 tbsp extra virgin olive oil
1 tsp lemon juice
pinch of salt

APPLE, CELERY, WALNUTS & POMEGRANATE SEEDS

For the salad, assemble:

50 g romaine lettuce
1 apple, chopped
2 celery stalks, sliced
handful of walnuts, chopped
handful of pomegranate seeds

For the dressing, mix:

1 tbsp extra virgin olive oil
1 tsp cider vinegar
pinch of salt and pepper
2 tbsp natural yoghurt

VEGAN

OMNIVORE ALTERNATIVE
Add some roasted chicken breast, or fried pancetta or chorizo

BARLEY, MUSHROOMS & GREEN BEANS

For the salad, assemble:

100 g pre-cooked barley
100 g pre-steamed green beans
100 g brown mushrooms, sliced
handful of fresh basil leaves

For the dressing, mix:

1 tbsp extra virgin olive oil
1 tsp balsamic vinegar
pinch of salt and pepper

PESCATARIAN

VEGAN
ALTERNATIVE
Replace the squid
with 100 g roasted
cauliflower

SQUID, SAFFRON, PEAS AND GIANT COUSCOUS

For the salad, assemble:

100 g pre-cooked giant Palestinian couscous
80 g pre-steamed peas
50 g pre-cooked squid, sliced
handful of fresh flat-leaf parsley leaves

For the dressing, mix:

1 tbsp extra virgin olive oil
1 tsp cider vinegar
pinch of salt and pepper
pinch of saffron threads

RAW

OMNIVORE
ALTERNATIVE
*Add 50 g roasted
chicken or smoked ham*

DATES, FENNEL & ALMONDS

For the salad, assemble:

1 little gem lettuce
1 small fennel, thinly sliced
handful of dried, pitted dates
handful of almonds, soaked in water for 10 minutes
handful of fresh dill fronds

For the dressing, mix:

1 tbsp extra virgin olive oil
1 tsp cider vinegar
pinch of salt and pepper
pinch of crushed fennel seeds

GORGONZOLA, CELERY, PISTACHIOS & PURSLANE

For the salad, assemble:

50 g winter purslane or watercress
2 celery stalks, sliced
handful of pistachios
50 g aged gorgonzola or other blue cheese, crumbled
handful of fresh flat-leaf parsley leaves

For the dressing, mix:

1 tbsp extra virgin olive oil
1 tsp balsamic vinegar
pinch of salt and pepper

OMNIVORE

OMNIVORE

VEGETARIAN ALTERNATIVE

Replace the chicken with 50 g goats' or blue cheese, or brie

ROASTED CHICKEN, COUSCOUS, PEAR & DRIED APRICOTS

For the salad, assemble:

100 g cooked wholewheat couscous
1 pear, chopped
handful of unsulphured dried apricots, chopped
50 g roasted chicken, chopped
handful of almonds, chopped
handful of fresh thyme leaves

For the dressing, mix:

1 tbsp extra virgin olive oil
1 tsp balsamic vinegar
pinch of salt and pepper

PECORINO, COUSCOUS, GREEN OLIVES & PICKLED ONIONS

For the salad, assemble:

100 g cooked wholewheat couscous
50 g young Pecorino, cubed
handful of baby pickled onions
handful of pitted green olives, halved
handful of fresh tarragon leaves

For the dressing, mix:

1 tbsp extra virgin olive oil
1 tsp cider vinegar
pinch of salt and pepper
pinch of chilli flakes

VEGETARIAN

VEGAN
ALTERNATIVE
*Replace the blue cheese
with your favourite tinned
beans, such as black-
eyed or cannellini*

QUINOA, BLUE CHEESE, CAVOLO NERO & ARTICHOKES

For the salad, assemble:

50 g cavolo nero, shredded (discard the stems)
½ fennel bulb, thinly sliced
50 g pre-cooked red and white quinoa
*small handful of grilled, marinated artichoke hearts,
   chopped*
50 g blue cheese, chopped
handful of pistachios
handful of fresh flat-leaf parsley leaves

For the dressing, mix:

1 tbsp extra virgin olive oil
1 tsp cider vinegar
pinch of salt and pepper

CHORIZO, ROASTED POTATOES & RED ONIONS

For the salad, assemble:

60 g cavolo nero, shredded (discard the stems)
100 g chopped and pre-roasted new potatoes
½ small red onion, thinly sliced
50 g chorizo, finely chopped

For the dressing, mix:

1 tbsp extra virgin olive oil
1 tsp cider vinegar
pinch of salt and pepper
pinch of smoked paprika

181

VEGAN

VEGETARIAN ALTERNATIVE

Add 50 g firm goats' cheese, Parmesan or Pecorino

CANNELLINI BEANS, MUSHROOMS & TRUFFLE CREAM

For the salad, assemble:

50 g watercress
100 g brown mushrooms, sliced
100 g tinned cannellini beans
handful of walnuts, chopped

For the dressing, mix:

1 tbsp extra virgin olive oil
1 tsp balsamic vinegar
1 tbsp soya or oat cream
1 tsp white truffle paste
1 tsp pre-ground walnuts

RICE, MUSHROOMS, PARMESAN & WATERCRESS

For the salad, assemble:

100 g pre-cooked white short-grain rice
100 g brown mushrooms, sliced
30 g watercress
2 spring onions, sliced
50 g Parmesan shavings

For the dressing, mix:

1 tbsp extra virgin olive oil
1 tsp balsamic vinegar
pinch of salt and pepper

RAW

PESCATARIAN
ALTERNATIVE
*Add 50 g marinated
anchovies*

BEETROOT, BLOOD ORANGE, RAISINS & RADICCHIO

For the salad, assemble:

100 g radicchio, shredded
1 small Sicilian blood orange, thinly sliced
1 beetroot, thinly sliced
handful of golden raisins
handful of pumpkin seeds
handful of fresh mint leaves

For the dressing, mix:

1 tbsp extra virgin olive oil
1 tsp cider vinegar
pinch of salt and pepper

SMOKED MACKEREL, ORANGE, KALE & BLACK OLIVES

For the salad, assemble:

60 g kale, chopped (discard the stems)
50 g smoked mackerel, flaked
handful of pitted black olives
1 orange, chopped

For the dressing, mix:

1 tbsp extra virgin olive oil
1 tsp lemon juice
pinch of salt and pepper

PESCATARIAN

VEGETARIAN
ALTERNATIVE
*Replace the crabmeat
with mild Cheddar or
Manchego*

CRABMEAT, BLACK QUINOA, EDAMAME & CARROT

For the salad, assemble:

100 g pre-cooked black quinoa
50 g pre-steamed edamame beans
1 carrot, shaved into ribbons with a vegetable peeler
50 g cooked crabmeat
handful of fresh coriander leaves

For the dressing, mix:

1 tbsp extra virgin olive oil
1 tsp cider vinegar
pinch of salt and pepper
1–2 chilli flakes

RAW

VEGETARIAN ALTERNATIVE
Add 50 g firm goats' cheese, brie or feta

FENNEL, CARROT, PISTACHIOS & GOJI BERRIES

For the salad, assemble:

50 g mixed baby salad leaves (e.g. chard and red oak leaf lettuce)
1 small carrot, shredded with a julienne peeler
1 small fennel bulb, thinly sliced
handful of dried goji berries
handful of pistachios
bunch of fresh chives, snipped

For the dressing, mix:

1 tbsp extra virgin olive oil
1 tsp cider vinegar
pinch of salt and pepper

ROASTED CHICKEN, PARSNIP & RED ONION

For the salad, assemble:

50 g rocket
1 chopped and pre-roasted parsnip
50 g roasted chicken, sliced
1 sliced and pre-roasted red onion
handful of pine nuts
handful of fresh thyme leaves

For the dressing, mix:

1 tbsp extra virgin olive oil
1 tsp balsamic vinegar
pinch of salt and pepper

WINTER

CELERY, CHICKPEAS, PUMPKIN SEEDS & MINT

For the salad, assemble:

2 celery stalks, sliced
100 g tinned chickpeas
handful of fresh mint leaves
handful of pumpkin seeds

For the dressing, blend together:

1 tbsp extra virgin olive oil
1 tsp cider vinegar
1 tbsp vegan cream (e.g. soya or oat)
pinch of salt and pepper

TALEGGIO, JERUSALEM ARTICHOKES & PINE NUTS

For the salad, assemble:

*50 g mixed baby salad leaves (e.g. chard, watercress
and red oak leaf lettuce)*
100 g chopped and pre-roasted Jerusalem artichokes
50 g Taleggio (or firm goats' cheese), cubed
handful of pine nuts
handful of fresh flat-leaf parsley leaves

For the dressing, mix:

1 tbsp extra virgin olive oil
1 tsp balsamic vinegar
pinch of salt and pepper

PASTRAMI, ROASTED SWEET POTATO & CAVOLO NERO

For the salad, assemble:

60 g cavolo nero, shredded (discard the stems)
½ pre-roasted sweet potato, cubed
handful of pre-steamed peas
50 g pastrami (or roasted beef), thinly sliced
handful of fresh mint leaves

For the dressing, mix:

1 tbsp extra virgin olive oil
1 tsp balsamic vinegar
pinch of salt and pepper

RAW

VEGETARIAN
ALTERNATIVE
*Add 50 g Parmesan,
Pecorino or firm
goats' cheese*

ROMANESCO, BEETROOT, APPLE & POMEGRANATE

For the salad, assemble:

100 g romanesco florets, chopped
1 apple, chopped
½ small beetroot, grated
handful of pomegranate seeds
handful of pumpkin seeds
handful of fresh flat-leaf parsley leaves

For the dressing, mix:

1 tbsp extra virgin olive oil
1 tsp cider vinegar
pinch of salt and pepper

PARSNIP, BEETROOT & GOATS' CHEESE

For the salad, assemble:

50 g watercress
1 small parsnip, shaved into ribbons with
    a vegetable peeler
½ small beetroot, cut into matchsticks
50 g firm goats' cheese, chopped
handful of pomegranate seeds
handful of pistachios
handful of fresh thyme leaves

For the dressing, mix:

1 tbsp extra virgin olive oil
1 tsp balsamic vinegar
pinch of salt and pepper

WHITE GRAPEFRUIT, KALE, APPLE & POMEGRANATE

For the salad, assemble:

50 g kale, chopped (discard the stems)
1 white grapefruit, chopped
1 apple, thinly sliced
handful of pomegranate seeds
handful of pumpkin seeds

For the dressing, mix:

1 tbsp extra virgin olive oil
1 tsp cider vinegar
pinch of salt and pepper

OMNIVORE

VEGAN ALTERNATIVE

Replace the roasted chicken with fennel, and add more walnuts

ROASTED CHICKEN, BLACK RICE & ORANGE

For the salad, assemble:

100 g pre-cooked black rice
1 orange, chopped
50 g roasted chicken breast, chopped
handful of walnuts, chopped
handful of raisins
bunch of fresh chives, snipped

For the dressing, mix:

1 tbsp extra virgin olive oil
1 tsp cider vinegar
pinch of salt and pepper
sprinkle of pared orange zest

ROASTED BUTTERNUT SQUASH & RED ONIONS, & CHICKPEAS

For the salad, assemble:

50 g rocket
100 g chopped and pre-roasted butternut squash
1 sliced and pre-roasted red onion
100 g tinned chickpeas

For the dressing, mix:

1 tbsp extra virgin olive oil
1 tsp balsamic vinegar
pinch of salt and pepper

SARDINES, PINTO BEANS & AVOCADO

For the salad, assemble:

1 little gem lettuce
1 small avocado, chopped
100 g tinned pinto beans (or borlotti beans)
50 g tinned sardines, flaked
2 spring onions, sliced

For the dressing, mix:

1 tbsp extra virgin olive oil
1 tsp lemon juice
pinch of salt and pepper

OMNIVORE

VEGETARIAN
ALTERNATIVE
*Simply omit the chorizo,
or add more Manchego
and roasted onion*

CHORIZO, CHILLI MANCHEGO & ROASTED SWEET POTATO

For the salad, assemble:

1 head of red chicory, shredded
1/2 pre-roasted sweet potato, chopped
1 sliced and pre-roasted red onion
50 g chorizo, cubed
50 g chilli Manchego (or scamorza smoked cheese), cubed
handful of fresh flat-leaf parsley leaves

For the dressing, mix:

1 tbsp extra virgin olive oil
1 tsp balsamic vinegar
pinch of salt and pepper

COUSCOUS, PECORINO, APPLE, PECANS & DATES

For the salad, assemble:

100 g cooked wholewheat couscous
1 apple, chopped
50 g young Pecorino (or smoked Cheddar), cubed
handful of dried, pitted dates, chopped
handful of pecans (or walnuts), chopped
1 tsp fresh thyme leaves

For the dressing, mix:

1 tbsp extra virgin olive oil
1 tsp lemon juice
pinch of salt and pepper

VEGAN

OMNIVORE
ALTERNATIVE
Add 50 g roasted chicken or beef

RED CABBAGE, MUSHROOMS & CARROT

For the salad, assemble:

100 g red cabbage, shredded
1 small (or regular) purple carrot, shaved into ribbons
  with a vegetable peeler
100 g brown mushrooms, sliced
1 tbsp sesame seeds
handful of fresh coriander leaves

For the dressing, mix:

1 tsp light soy sauce
pinch of salt and pepper
2 tbsp soya cream
1 tsp chilli power

GOATS' CHEESE, PEAR, CARROT & HAZELNUTS

For the salad, assemble:

1 big carrot, shaved into ribbons with a vegetable peeler
1 pear, chopped
50 g goats' cheese, crumbled
handful of blanched hazelnuts, chopped
handful of pomegranate seeds
handful of fresh thyme leaves

For the dressing, mix:

1 tbsp extra virgin olive oil
1 tsp balsamic vinegar
pinch of salt and pepper

RAW

PESCATARIAN ALTERNATIVE
Add 50 g smoked mackerel

CELERY, RADISH, BEETROOT & RAW HORSERADISH CREAM

For the salad, assemble:

2 celery stalks, sliced
handful of radishes, chopped
1 small beetroot, grated
handful of dried blueberries
handful of pine nuts
bunch of fresh chives, snipped

For the dressing, blend together:

50 g freshly grated horseradish root
1 tsp cider vinegar
pinch of salt
60 ml water (or more if needed to facilitate blending)
2 tbsp extra virgin olive oil

PESCATARIAN

VEGAN ALTERNATIVE
Replace the trout with ½ roasted sweet potato, and replace the dressing with the one opposite

QUINOA, SMOKED TROUT & BEETROOT

For the salad, assemble:

100 g pre-cooked red and white quinoa
1 beetroot, very thinly sliced (or shaved with a vegetable peeler)
50 g smoked trout, flaked
bunch of fresh chives, trimmed

For the dressing, mix:

1 tbsp extra virgin olive oil
1 tsp cider vinegar
pinch of salt and pepper
1 tsp horseradish sauce

VEGAN

OMNIVORE
ALTERNATIVE
*Add some fried pancetta
cubes or chorizo*

COUSCOUS, BLACK BEANS, CHICORY & POMEGRANATE

For the salad, assemble:

100 g cooked wholewheat couscous
1 head of red chicory, chopped
50 g tinned black beans
handful of pomegranate seeds
bunch of fresh chives, snipped

For the dressing, mix:

1 tbsp extra virgin olive oil
1 tsp balsamic vinegar
pinch of salt and pepper

PESCATARIAN

**VEGAN
ALTERNATIVE**
*Replace the salmon
caviar with 100 g
edamame beans or
1 avocado*

SALMON CAVIAR, JASMINE RICE, CUCUMBER & NORI

For the salad, assemble:

100 g pre-cooked jasmine rice
100 g cucumber, chopped
handful of shredded nori (toasted seaweed)
2 spring onions, sliced
2 tbsp salmon caviar

For the dressing, mix:

1 tbsp toasted sesame oil
1 tsp dark soy sauce
pinch of salt

VEGAN

PESCATARIAN
ALTERNATIVE
*Add 50 g tinned tuna
(preserved in water)*

ROASTED POTATOES, BLACK OLIVES & CAPERS

For the salad, assemble:

50 g lettuce, such as frisée
2 pre-roasted potatoes, chopped
1 tbsp pitted black olives, halved
2 spring onions, sliced
1 tbsp capers

For the dressing, mix:

1 tbsp extra virgin olive oil
1 tsp cider vinegar
pinch of salt and pepper

OMNIVORE ALTERNATIVE
Replace the salmon with 50 g roasted beef or smoked ham

ROASTED SALMON & POTATOES, BLACK QUINOA & PARSNIP

For the salad, assemble:

*1 parsnip, shaved into ribbons with
  a vegetable peeler
100 g halved pre-roasted new potatoes
50 g pre-cooked black quinoa
50 g pre-roasted salmon, flaked
handful of fresh flat-leaf parsley leaves*

For the dressing, mix:

*1 tbsp extra virgin olive oil
1 tsp balsamic vinegar
pinch of salt and pepper*

HAM, ROASTED POTATOES, CARROT & DRIED CRANBERRIES

For the salad, assemble:

*1 big carrot, shaved into ribbons with
   a vegetable peeler*
30 g rocket
3 halved and pre-roasted new potatoes
handful of dried cranberries
50 g ham, thinly sliced
handful of fresh flat-leaf parsley leaves

For the dressing, mix:

1 tbsp extra virgin olive oil
1 tsp balsamic vinegar
pinch of salt and pepper

VEGAN

PESCATARIAN
ALTERNATIVE
Add 50 g tinned tuna
(preserved in water),
sardines or anchovies,
and some parsley

ROASTED POTATOES, CHERRY TOMATOES & CHILLI

For the salad, assemble:

100 g halved and pre-steamed new potatoes,
tossed with olive oil and finely chopped parsley
200 g cherry tomatoes, halved
1 small red onion, thinly sliced
handful of capers
1 small chilli, thinly sliced

For the dressing, mix:

1 tbsp extra virgin olive oil
1 tsp cider vinegar
pinch of salt and pepper

RAW

VEGETARIAN
ALTERNATIVE
*Add 50 g blue cheese or
goats' cheese*

KALE, APPLE & DRIED APRICOTS

For the salad, assemble:

80 g kale, chopped (discard the stems)
1 apple, chopped
handful of unsulphured dried apricots, chopped
handful of pine nuts

For the dressing, mix:

1 tbsp extra virgin olive oil
1 tsp cider vinegar
pinch of salt and pepper

PESCATARIAN

OMINIVORE
ALTERNATIVE
*Replace the tuna with
50 g roasted beef or
smoked ham*

QUAIL EGGS, TUNA, KALE & CELERY

For the salad, assemble:

50 g kale, chopped (discard the stems)
3 celery stalks, sliced
6 hard-boiled quail eggs
50 g tinned tuna (preserved in water), flaked
bunch of fresh chives, snipped

For the dressing, mix:

1 tbsp extra virgin olive oil
1 tsp cider vinegar
pinch of celery salt
2 tbsp mayonnaise

ROASTED TURKEY, MUSHROOMS, CARROT & WALNUTS

For the salad, assemble:

50 g mixed salad leaves (e.g. chard and spinach)
1 small carrot, shaved into ribbons with a
   vegetable peeler
handful of (fresh or pre-roasted) brown mushrooms,
   sliced
50 g roasted turkey, sliced
handful of walnuts
bunch of fresh chives, snipped

For the dressing, mix:

1 tbsp extra virgin olive oil
1 tsp cider vinegar
pinch of salt and pepper

ROASTED SWEET POTATO, BROCCOLI & CARROT

For the salad, assemble:

½ pre-roasted sweet potato, chopped
*1 big carrot, shaved into ribbons with a
    vegetable peeler*
100 g raw or pre-steamed broccoli florets, chopped
2 spring onions, sliced
handful of fresh flat-leaf parsley leaves
handful of pine nuts

For the dressing, mix:

1 tbsp extra virgin olive oil
1 tsp cider vinegar
pinch of salt and pepper

VEGAN

VEGETARIAN ALTERNATIVE

Add 50 g cheese, such as ricotta or cottage cheese

ROASTED SWEET POTATO, BLACK LENTILS & PISTACHIOS

For the salad, assemble:

50 g mixed baby salad leaves (e.g. chard, watercress and red oak leaf lettuce)
50 g tinned black (or green) lentils
½ pre-roasted sweet potato, cut into wedges
2 spring onions, sliced
handful of pistachios

For the dressing, mix:

1 tbsp extra virgin olive oil
1 tsp balsamic vinegar
pinch of salt and pepper

BLACK RICE, ROASTED SWEET POTATO & PECORINO

For the salad, assemble:

100 g pre-cooked black rice
handful of semi-dried tomatoes
½ pre-roasted sweet potato, chopped
50 g Pecorino shavings
handful of pine nuts
handful of fresh basil leaves

For the dressing, mix:

1 tbsp extra virgin olive oil
1 tsp balsamic vinegar
pinch of salt and pepper

VEGETARIAN ALTERNATIVE

Omit the water and cashew nuts from the dressing; replace with natural yoghurt

FENNEL, APPLE, CELERY AND CASHEW CREAM

For the salad, assemble:

½ fennel bulb, thinly sliced
½ apple, cut into wedges
1 celery stalk, sliced
handful of pomegranate seeds
handful of raisins
handful of pumpkin seeds
sprinkle of fresh thyme leaves

For the dressing, blend together:

1 tbsp extra virgin olive oil
1 tsp cider vinegar
pinch of salt
1 tbsp water
handful of cashew nuts

VEGETARIAN

RAW ALTERNATIVE
Replace the blue cheese with Nut & Lemon dressing (page 26, made with walnuts)

BLUE CHEESE, APPLE, CAULIFLOWER & WALNUTS

For the salad, assemble:

1 apple, chopped
100 g cauliflower florets, chopped
50 g blue cheese, chopped
handful of walnuts
bunch of fresh chives, snipped

For the dressing, mix:

1 tbsp extra virgin olive oil
1 tsp cider vinegar
pinch of salt and pepper

VEGAN

OMNIVORE ALTERNATIVE
Add 50 g roasted chicken (or prawns)

BARLEY, ROASTED SWEET POTATO & EDAMAME

For the salad, assemble:

100 g pre-cooked barley
50 g cavolo nero, shredded (discard the stems)
½ pre-roasted sweet potato, chopped
50 g pre-steamed edamame beans
bunch of fresh chives, snipped

For the dressing, mix:

1 tbsp extra virgin olive oil
1 tsp balsamic vinegar
pinch of salt and pepper

ROASTED SWEET POTATO & CHICKEN, & BROWN RICE

For the salad, assemble:

100 g pre-cooked brown short-grain rice
30 g green or savoy cabbage, shredded
½ pre-roasted sweet potato, chopped
50 g roasted chicken, sliced
handful of almonds, chopped
bunch of fresh chives, snipped

For the dressing, mix:

1 tbsp extra virgin olive oil
1 tsp cider vinegar
pinch of salt and pepper
1 tbsp Dijon wholegrain mustard

RAW
ALTERNATIVE

*Replace the Parma
ham with more pine
nuts, and a handful of
walnuts and raisins*

PARMA HAM, PEAR & PINE NUTS

For the salad, assemble:

*50 g mixed salad leaves (e.g. watercress, rocket and
red oak leaf lettuce)*
1 pear, chopped
50 g Parma ham, thinly sliced
handful of pine nuts

For the dressing, mix:

1 tbsp extra virgin olive oil
1 tsp balsamic vinegar
pinch of salt and pepper

RAW

VEGETARIAN ALTERNATIVE

Add 50 g blue cheese, such as Stilton or Gorgonzola piccante

PEAR, DATES, CASHEW NUTS & CHICORY

For the salad, assemble:

1 head of chicory
1 big pear, chopped
handful of dried, pitted dates, halved
handful of cashew nuts
bunch of fresh chives, trimmed

For the dressing, mix:

1 tbsp extra virgin olive oil
1 tsp lemon juice
pinch of salt and pepper

CANNELLINI BEANS, PECORINO, PINE NUTS & WATERCRESS

For the salad, assemble:

50 g watercress
100 g tinned cannellini beans
handful of fresh basil leaves
handful of pine nuts
50 g Pecorino shavings

For the dressing, mix:

1 tbsp extra virgin olive oil
1 tsp balsamic vinegar
pinch of salt and pepper
2 tbsp Classic Pesto (page 25)

NEW POTATOES, PEAS & RED LETTUCE

For the salad, assemble:

50 g baby red lettuce
100 g halved and pre-steamed new potatoes
100 g pre-steamed peas
handful of fresh flat-leaf parsley leaves

For the dressing, blend together:

1 tsp extra virgin olive oil
1 tsp cider vinegar
1 tbsp vegan cream (e.g. soya or oat)
pinch of salt and pepper
1 tbsp of capers

PESCATARIAN

VEGETARIAN ALTERNATIVE
Replace the tuna with 50 g goats' cheese, brie or Pecorino

TUNA, COUSCOUS, KALE, GREEN LENTILS & RED ONION

For the salad, assemble:

100 g cooked wholewheat couscous
60 g kale, chopped (discard the stems)
100 g tinned green lentils
50 g tinned tuna (preserved in water), flaked
1 sliced and pre-roasted red onion

For the dressing, mix:

1 tbsp extra virgin olive oil
1 tsp lemon juice
pinch of salt and pepper

PASTRAMI, CORNICHONS & CROUTONS

For the salad, assemble:

70 g mixed salad leaves (e.g. wild rocket)
handful of cornichons (cocktail gherkins)
50 g pastrami, thinly sliced
handful of wholewheat croutons

For the dressing, mix:

1 tbsp extra virgin olive oil
1 tsp cider vinegar
pinch of salt and pepper
1 tsp English mustard
1 tbsp single cream

PESCATARIAN

VEGAN
ALTERNATIVE
*Replace the anchovies
with 100 g roasted
parsnip*

ANCHOVIES, BORLOTTI BEANS & ROCKET

For the salad, assemble:

50 g rocket
100 g tinned borlotti beans
50 g marinated anchovies
handful of pine nuts
handful of fresh flat-leaf parsley leaves

For the dressing, mix:

1 tbsp extra virgin olive oil
1 tsp cider vinegar
pinch of salt and pepper

RAW

VEGETARIAN ALTERNATIVE
Add 50 g natural or Greek yoghurt

RASPBERRIES, RED CABBAGE & FENNEL

For the salad, assemble:

80 g red cabbage, shredded
1 small fennel bulb, thinly sliced
handful of raspberries
handful of pumpkin seeds
handful of fresh mint leaves

For the dressing, mix:

1 tbsp extra virgin olive oil
1 tsp lemon juice
pinch of salt and pepper

SASHIMI TUNA, PINK GRAPEFRUIT & CHILLI

For the salad, assemble:

50 g rocket
50 g sashimi tuna, very thinly sliced
½ big pink grapefruit, chopped
1 small red onion, finely chopped
1 small red chilli, deseeded and finely chopped
1 tbsp toasted sesame seeds

For the dressing, mix:

1 tbsp extra virgin olive oil
1 tsp lemon juice
pinch of salt and pepper

RAW

PESCATARIAN ALTERNATIVE
Add 50 g cooked prawns or smoked mackerel

PINK GRAPEFRUIT, AVOCADO & CABBAGE

For the salad, assemble:

80 g green cabbage, shredded
1 ripe avocado, chopped
½ big pink grapefruit, chopped
handful of pine nuts
handful of pomegranate seeds

For the dressing, mix:

1 tbsp extra virgin olive oil
1 tsp lemon juice
pinch of salt and pepper

RAW

OMNIVORE ALTERNATIVE
Add 50 g roasted chicken, Parma ham or another cured ham

PEAR, ORANGE, RED CABBAGE & POPPY SEEDS

For the salad, assemble:

100 g red cabbage, shredded
1 pear, chopped
1 orange, chopped
handful of walnuts
1 tbsp poppy seeds
handful of fresh flat-leaf parsley leaves

For the dressing, mix:

1 tbsp extra virgin olive oil
1 tsp lemon juice
pinch of salt and pepper

OMNIVORE

RAW ALTERNATIVE
Replace the beef with a handful of walnuts, and the dressing with Raw Nut & Agave (page 27)

ROASTED BEEF, CAULIFLOWER & RED CABBAGE

For the salad, assemble:

60 g red cabbage, shredded
100 g cauliflower florets, chopped
50 g roast beef, thinly sliced
handful of dried cranberries
handful of pine nuts
handful of fresh flat-leaf parsley leaves

For the dressing, mix:

2 tbsp extra virgin olive oil
1 tsp cider vinegar
pinch of salt and pepper
1 tsp single cream
1 tsp Dijon mustard

SPRING

PARMA HAM, ENOKI MUSHROOMS & ASPARAGUS

For the salad, assemble:

*1 small parsnip, shaved into ribbons with
  a vegetable peeler*
*3 asparagus spears, shaved into ribbons with
  a vegetable peeler*
50 g purple sprouting broccoli florets, chopped
handful of enoki mushrooms
50 g Parma ham, thinly sliced
handful of toasted hazelnuts, chopped
handful of fresh basil leaves

For the dressing, mix:

1 tbsp extra virgin olive oil
1 tsp balsamic vinegar
pinch of salt and pepper

RAW

VEGETARIAN ALTERNATIVE

Replace the water with single cream or natural yoghurt

PARSNIP, PINK GRAPEFRUIT & POPPY SEEDS

For the salad, assemble:

1 parsnip, shaved into ribbons with a vegetable peeler
1 pink grapefruit (or blood orange), chopped
handful of raisins
sprinkle of poppy seeds
handful of fresh mint leaves

For the dressing, blend together:

1 tsp lemon juice
2 tbsp desiccated coconut
2 tbsp water
pinch of salt
½ tsp ground ginger

CAULIFLOWER, GREEN BEANS & SPINACH

For the salad, assemble:

50 g baby spinach
100 g cauliflower florets, chopped
100 g pre-steamed green beans
handful of pine nuts
50 g Pecorino shavings
handful of fresh basil leaves

For the dressing, mix:

1 tbsp extra virgin olive oil
1 tsp balsamic vinegar
2 tbsp Classic Pesto (page 25)
pinch of salt and pepper

PESCATARIAN

VEGAN ALTERNATIVE
Replace the mackerel with tinned black beans or lentils, or green beans

SMOKED MACKEREL, KALE & MARINATED PEPPERS

For the salad, assemble:

50 g chopped and pre-steamed kale (or raw and
    massaged with lemon juice and left for 5 minutes)
handful of marinated red peppers from a jar, chopped
50 g smoked mackerel, flaked
handful of crispy onions
handful of fresh flat-leaf parsley leaves

For the dressing, mix:

1 tbsp extra virgin olive oil
1 tsp lemon juice
pinch of salt and pepper

RAW

OMNIVORE
ALTERNATIVE
*Add 100 g roasted
chicken or beef*

CARROT, RED ONION, WALNUTS & RAISINS

For the salad, assemble:

50 g lamb's lettuce
*1 carrot, shaved into ribbons with
  a vegetable peeler*
½ small red onion, thinly sliced
handful of raisins
handful of walnuts, chopped

For the dressing, mix:

1 tbsp extra virgin olive oil
1 tsp cider vinegar
pinch of salt and pepper
1 tbsp mustard seeds, pre-soaked overnight

VEGAN

VEGETARIAN ALTERNATIVE
Add 50 g cheese, such as goats' cheese, Manchego or blue cheese

QUINOA, ROASTED SWEET POTATO & CAULIFLOWER

For the salad, assemble:

100 g pre-cooked red and white quinoa
50 g radicchio, shredded
½ pre-roasted sweet potato, chopped
100 g cauliflower florets, chopped
handful of fresh flat-leaf parsley leaves

For the dressing, mix:

1 tbsp extra virgin olive oil
1 tsp cider vinegar
pinch of salt
pinch of crushed fennel seeds

VEGAN

VEGETARIAN ALTERNATIVE
Add 50 g feta, Parmesan or Pecorino

ROASTED POTATOES & SUN-DRIED TOMATOES

For the salad, assemble:

70 g mixed baby salad leaves (e.g. watercress, chard and red oak leaf lettuce)
2 pre-roasted potatoes, chopped
handful of sun-dried tomatoes, chopped
2 spring onions, sliced

For the dressing, mix:

1 tbsp extra virgin olive oil
1 tsp cider vinegar
pinch of salt and pepper
pinch of chilli flakes

ROASTED BEEF, CABBAGE & MARINATED PEPPERS

For the salad, assemble:

100 g white cabbage, shredded
¼ red onion, finely chopped
50 g marinated peppers from a jar, chopped
handful of pitted kalamata olives
50 g roasted beef, thinly sliced
sprinkle of garlic sprouts
handful of pine nuts

For the dressing, mix:

1 tbsp extra virgin olive oil
1 tsp balsamic vinegar
pinch of salt and pepper

241

PESCATARIAN

**VEGAN
ALTERNATIVE**
*Replace the prawns with
100 g steamed broccoli*

PRAWNS, AVOCADO & RED CAMARGUE RICE

For the salad, assemble:

100 g pre-cooked red Camargue rice
30 g rocket
1 avocado, chopped
50 g cooked prawns
2 spring onions, sliced
sprinkle of sesame seeds

For the dressing, mix:

1 tbsp extra virgin olive oil
pinch of salt
1 tbsp mayonnaise
pinch of ground saffron
pinch of ground turmeric

MANGO, MANGETOUT, PAK CHOI & BROCCOLI

For the salad, assemble:

70 g pak choi or spring greens, finely chopped
handful of mangetout or sugar snap peas
100 g broccoli florets, chopped
100 g mango, cubed
2 spring onions, sliced
handful of fresh basil leaves

For the dressing, mix:

1 tbsp extra virgin olive oil
1 tsp cider vinegar
pinch of salt
pinch of chilli flakes

OMNIVORE

ROASTED BEEF, BLACK LENTILS & MUSHROOMS

For the salad, assemble:

60 g watercress
100 g tinned black lentils
handful of brown mushrooms, sliced
50 g roasted beef, thinly sliced
bunch of fresh chives, snipped

For the dressing, mix:

1 tbsp extra virgin olive oil
1 tbsp truffle-infused olive oil
1 tsp balsamic vinegar
pinch of salt and pepper

QUINOA, EGG, MANCHEGO, BLACK OLIVES & PICKLES

For the salad, assemble:

100 g pre-cooked red and white quinoa
1 hard-boiled egg, chopped
small handful of pitted black olives, halved
50 g Manchego, Cheddar or other mild cheese, chopped
4–6 cornichons
4–6 baby pickled onions
handful of fresh flat-leaf parsley leaves

For the dressing, mix:

1 tbsp extra virgin olive oil
1 tsp balsamic vinegar
pinch of salt and pepper

VEGETARIAN

OMNIVORE
ALTERNATIVE
*Add 50 g roasted
chicken, or chorizo*

CHEDDAR, BLACK BEANS & SUN-DRIED TOMATOES

For the salad, assemble:

60 g white cabbage, shredded
100 g tinned black beans
½ small red onion, finely chopped
handful of sun-dried tomatoes, chopped
50 g mature Cheddar, cubed
handful of fresh coriander leaves

For the dressing, mix:

1 tbsp extra virgin olive oil
1 tsp cider vinegar
pinch of salt
pinch of chilli flakes

RAW

OMNIVORE
ALTERNATIVE
*Add 50 g roasted
chicken or beef, or ham*

PARSNIP, ASPARAGUS, PINE NUTS & RAW PESTO

For the salad, assemble:

*3 asparagus spears, shaved into ribbons with
   a vegetable peeler*
*1 parsnip (or carrot), shaved into ribbons with
   a vegetable peeler*
handful of pine nuts
handful of fresh flat-leaf parsley leaves

For the dressing, mix:

1 tbsp extra virgin olive oil
1 tsp cider vinegar
pinch of salt and pepper
2 tbsp Raw Green Pesto (page 25)

ROASTED SWEET POTATO, QUINOA & COTTAGE CHEESE

For the salad, assemble:

50 g spring greens, shredded
100 g pre-cooked red quinoa
½ pre-roasted sweet potato, chopped
2 tbsp cottage cheese
handful of fresh flat-leaf parsley leaves

For the dressing, mix:

1 tbsp extra virgin olive oil
1 tsp cider vinegar
pinch of salt and pepper

ROASTED SWEET POTATO, BUTTER BEANS & PISTACHIOS

For the salad, assemble:

50 g pea shoots or watercress
100 g tinned butter or broad beans
½ pre-roasted sweet potato, chopped
handful of pistachios

For the dressing, mix:

1 tbsp extra virgin olive oil
1 tsp cider vinegar
pinch of salt and pepper

RAW

VEGETARIAN ALTERNATIVE
Replace the Raw Nut & Agave dressing with double cream

CAULIFLOWER, AVOCADO & GOJI BERRIES

For the salad, assemble:

50 g lamb's lettuce
50 g cauliflower florets, chopped
1 avocado, chopped
handful of dried goji berries
handful of pine nuts

For the dressing, mix:

1 tbsp extra virgin olive oil
1 tsp cider vinegar
pinch of salt and pepper
pinch of saffron threads
2 tbsp Raw Nut & Agave dressing
(page 27, made with pine nuts)

PESCATARIAN

RAW ALTERNATIVE

Replace the prawns with a handful of cashew nuts; and the soy sauce with lemon juice in the dressing

PRAWNS, MANGO, SPRING ONIONS & CHILLI

For the salad, assemble:

70 g mixed salad leaves
½ small mango, cubed
handful of cooked prawns
2 spring onions, sliced
handful of fresh coriander leaves

For the dressing, mix:

1 tbsp sunflower oil
1 tsp light soy sauce (or Thai fish sauce)
pinch of salt and pepper
pinch of chilli flakes

VEGETARIAN

OMNIVORE
ALTERNATIVE
*Add 50 g roasted
chicken or beef*

BROWN RICE, MOZZARELLA & MUSHROOMS

For the salad, assemble:

100 g pre-cooked brown short-grain rice
100 g chopped and pre-roasted brown mushrooms
50 g mozzarella, chopped
handful of fresh basil leaves

For the dressing, mix:

1 tbsp extra virgin olive oil
1 tsp cider vinegar
pinch of salt and pepper

OMNIVORE

VEGAN
ALTERNATIVE
*Replace the chicken
with a further 50 g broad
beans*

ROASTED CHICKEN, QUINOA, BROAD BEANS & CORN

For the salad, assemble:

100 g pre-cooked red and white quinoa
1 small avocado, chopped
50 g fresh or tinned sweetcorn
50 g pre-steamed broad beans
50 g roasted chicken, chopped
handful of fresh coriander leaves

For the dressing, mix:

1 tbsp extra virgin olive oil
2 tbsp soya cream
1 tbsp ground ginger
pinch of salt and pepper

PESCATARIAN

OMNIVORE
ALTERNATIVE

*Replace the mackerel
with 50 g roasted beef or
ham; add 1 tsp Dijon
mustard to the
dressing*

SMOKED MACKEREL, ROASTED POTATOES & KALE

For the salad, assemble:

50 g kale, chopped (discard the stems)
3 pre-roasted potatoes, chopped
handful of dried cranberries
100 g smoked mackerel, flaked
2 spring onions, sliced

For the dressing, mix:

1 tbsp extra virgin olive oil
1 tsp lemon juce
pinch of salt and pepper

VEGAN

RAW ALTERNATIVE
Replace the black beans with a handful of cashew nuts

BLACK BEANS, AVOCADO, SHALLOT & CHILLI

For the salad, assemble:

50 g lamb's lettuce
100 g tinned black beans
1 avocado, chopped
1 small shallot, thinly sliced
1 small red chilli, deseeded and finely chopped
handful of fresh flat-leaf parsley leaves

For the dressing, mix:

1 tbsp extra virgin olive oil
1 tsp lemon juice
pinch of salt and pepper

COUSCOUS, BLACK LENTILS & PISTACHIOS

For the salad, assemble:

*100 g couscous cooked with a pinch of dried parsley
   and coriander*
100 g tinned black lentils
handful of pistachios
handful of fresh coriander leaves

For the dressing, mix:

1 tbsp extra virgin olive oil
1 tsp cider vinegar
pinch of salt and pepper
2 tbsp vegan lemon and coriander houmous

RAW

PESCATARIAN ALTERNATIVE

Add 50 g smoked mackerel and 1 small avocado

PINK GRAPEFUIT, BROCCOLI, KALE & CAPERS

For the salad, assemble:

50 g kale, chopped (discard the stems)
100 g purple sprouting broccoli florets, chopped
1 pink grapefruit, chopped
1 tbsp capers
handful of almonds, chopped

For the dressing, mix:

1 tbsp extra virgin olive oil
1 tsp lemon juice
pinch of salt and pepper

CARROT, ORANGE, DRIED APRICOTS & PISTACHIOS

For the salad, assemble:

2 small carrots, shredded with a julienne peeler
1 orange, chopped
handful of unsulphured dried apricots, chopped
handful of pistachios
sprinkle of pared lemon zest
handful of fresh mint leaves

For the dressing, mix:

1 tbsp extra virgin olive oil
1 tsp lemon juice
pinch of salt and pepper
2 tbsp Nut & Lemon dressing (page 26, made with cashew nuts)

PESCATARIAN

OMNIVORE ALTERNATIVE

Replace the smoked mackerel with smoked ham

SMOKED MACKEREL, PURPLE CARROT & AVOCADO

For the salad, assemble:

*1 purple (or regular) carrot, shaved into ribbons with
a vegetable peeler*
½ avocado, chopped
handful of semi-dried tomatoes
50 g smoked mackerel, flaked
handful of pine nuts
1 tbsp poppy seeds
handful of fresh lemon thyme leaves

For the dressing, mix:

1 tbsp extra virgin olive oil
1 tsp balsamic vinegar
pinch of salt and pepper

VEGAN

OMNIVORE
ALTERNATIVE
*Add 50 g roasted
chicken, or chorizo*

QUINOA, SUN-DRIED TOMATOES, PARSNIP & CRISPY ONIONS

For the salad, assemble:

*1 big parsnip, shaved into ribbons with
   a vegetable peeler*
100 g pre-cooked red and white quinoa
1 tbsp crispy onions
50 g sun-dried tomatoes
handful of fresh basil leaves

For the dressing, mix:

1 tbsp extra virgin olive oil
1 tsp balsamic vinegar
pinch of salt and pepper

VEGAN ALTERNATIVE

Replace the salmon with 100 g tinned kidney, borlotti or aduki beans

ROASTED SALMON, QUINOA, PARSNIP & CAVOLO NERO

For the salad, assemble:

60 g cavolo nero, shredded (discard the stems)
50 g pre-cooked black quinoa
1 small parsnip, shaved into ribbons with
*   a vegetable peeler*
50 g marinated red peppers from a jar, chopped
150 g roasted salmon, flaked
handful of fresh flat-leaf parsley leaves

For the dressing, mix:

1 tbsp extra virgin olive oil
1 tsp balsamic vinegar
pinch of salt and pepper

VEGETARIAN

VEGAN ALTERNATIVE
Replace the blue cheese with 100 g tinned green or black lentils

CAULIFLOWER, BLUE CHEESE & MARINATED PEPPERS

For the salad, assemble:

30 g rocket
100 g cauliflower florets, chopped
handful of marinated red and yellow peppers from a jar
50 g blue cheese, crumbled
handful of pumpkin seeds
bunch of fresh chives, trimmed

For the dressing, mix:

1 tbsp extra virgin olive oil
1 tsp balsamic vinegar
pinch of salt and pepper

RAW ALTERNATIVE

Replace the roasted salmon artichokes with cherry tomatoes and pecan nuts

ROASTED SALMON, CAULIFLOWER & ARTICHOKES

For the salad, assemble:

100 g cauliflower florets, finely chopped
handful of grilled, marinated artichoke hearts,
*   chopped*
50 g roasted salmon, flaked
2 spring onions, sliced
1 tbsp poppy seeds
handful of fresh coriander leaves

For the dressing, mix:

1 tbsp extra virgin olive oil
1 tsp lemon juice
pinch of salt and pepper

RAW

VEGAN
ALTERNATIVE
*Add 100 g tinned
butter beans or
black-eyed peas*

SUN-DRIED TOMATOES, AVOCADO & RADICCHIO

For the salad, assemble:

50 g radicchio
1 avocado, chopped
50 g sun-dried tomatoes
handful of pine nuts
1 small shallot, thinly sliced
handful of fresh flat-leaf parsley leaves

For the dressing, mix:

1 tbsp extra virgin olive oil
1 tsp lemon juice
pinch of salt and pepper

VEGAN

OMNIVORE ALTERNATIVE
Add 50 g chorizo, ham or roasted beef

CHICKPEAS, BLACK OLIVES & SUN-DRIED TOMATOES

For the salad, assemble:

50 g red oak leaf lettuce
100 g tinned chickpeas
50 g sun-dried tomatoes
handful of pitted black olives, halved
1 tbsp toasted sesame seeds
handful of fresh flat-leaf parsley leaves

For the dressing, mix:

1 tbsp extra virgin olive oil
1 tsp lemon juice
pinch of salt and pepper
2 tbsp vegan houmous

265

GRILLED SQUID, AVOCADO, EDAMAME & CHILLI

For the salad, assemble:

50 g rocket
1 avocado, chopped
50 g pre-steamed edamame beans
50 g pre-grilled squid, sliced
1 small red chilli, deseeded and chopped
handful of fresh coriander leaves

For the dressing, mix:

1 tbsp extra virgin olive oil
1 tsp lemon juice
pinch of salt and pepper
couple of pinches of ground ginger

OMNIVORE

RAW
ALTERNATIVE
*Replace the chicken
with cashew nuts, and the
soya cream with Raw
Nut & Agave
(page 27)*

ROASTED CHICKEN, YELLOW CARROT & PURPLE BROCCOLI

For the salad, assemble:

50 g spring greens, chopped
*1 small yellow (or regular) carrot, shaved into ribbons
    with a vegetable peeler*
½ avocado, chopped
50 g purple sprouting broccoli florets, chopped
50 g roasted chicken, sliced
handful of fresh flat-leaf parsley leaves

For the dressing, mix:

1 tbsp extra virgin olive oil
2 tbsp soya cream
1 tbsp ground ginger
pinch of salt and pepper

VEGETARIAN

OMNIVORE
ALTERNATIVE
*Add some pan-fried
pancetta cubes or chorizo*

PASTA, GREEN BEANS, KALE & COTTAGE CHEESE

For the salad, assemble:

100 g pre-cooked wholewheat fusilli
40 g kale, chopped (discard the stems)
handful of pre-steamed green beans
handful of sun-dried tomatoes
50 g cottage cheese
handful of fresh basil leaves

For the dressing, mix:

1 tbsp extra virgin olive oil
1 tsp balsamic vinegar
pinch of salt and pepper

WILD RICE, CAULIFLOWER & SPRING GREENS

For the salad, assemble:

100 g pre-cooked wild rice
30 g spring greens, finely chopped
100 g cauliflower florets, chopped
bunch of fresh chives, snipped

For the dressing, blend together:

1 tbsp sun-dried tomatoes
1 tbsp extra virgin olive oil
1 tsp cider vinegar
pinch of salt and pepper
pinch of chilli flakes
1 tsp water

VEGAN

OMNIVORE
ALTERNATIVE
Add 50 g smoked ham

RED CABBAGE, BLACK LENTILS & CARROT

For the salad, assemble:

100 g tinned black lentils
100 g red cabbage, shredded
1 carrot, shaved into ribbons with a vegetable peeler
handful of pine nuts
bunch of fresh chives, trimmed

For the dressing, blend together:

1 tbsp sun-dried tomatoes
1 tbsp extra virgin olive oil
1 tsp cider vinegar
pinch of salt and pepper
1 tsp water

VEGETARIAN

VEGAN ALTERNATIVE
Replace the goats' cheese with 100 g tomatoes or ½ roasted sweet potato

GOATS' CHEESE, BROWN LENTILS & PINE NUTS

For the salad, assemble:

50 g mixed salad leaves (e.g. frisée, lamb's lettuce and radicchio)
100 g tinned brown lentils
50 g firm goats' cheese or brie, chopped
handful of pine nuts
bunch of fresh chives, snipped

For the dressing, mix:

1 tbsp extra virgin olive oil
1 tsp cider vinegar
pinch of salt and pepper
pinch of ground cumin

OMNIVORE

PESCATARIAN ALTERNATIVE

Replace the roasted chicken with 50 g roasted salmon

ROASTED CHICKEN, BROWN RICE & BLACK BEANS

For the salad, assemble:

100 g pre-cooked brown short-grain rice
100 g tinned black beans
50 g marinated red peppers from a jar, chopped
50 g roasted chicken, sliced
handful of pumpkin seeds
handful of fresh mint leaves

For the dressing, mix:

1 tbsp extra virgin olive oil
1 tsp balsamic vinegar
pinch of salt and pepper
pinch of smoked paprika

SASHIMI SALMON, AVOCADO & JASMINE RICE

For the salad, assemble:

100 g pre-cooked jasmine rice
handful of baby watercress
1 avocado, chopped
50 g sashimi salmon, thinly sliced
bunch of fresh chives, trimmed

For the dressing, mix:

2 tbsp toasted sesame (or sunflower) oil
2 tsp dark soy sauce
1 tbsp wasabi powder

ROASTED BUTTERNUT SQUASH, BLACK LENTILS & CABBAGE

For the salad, assemble:

100 g white cabbage, shredded
100 g chopped and pre-roasted butternut squash
100 g tinned black lentils
1 tbsp sesame seeds
1 tbsp fresh thyme leaves

For the dressing, mix:

1 tbsp extra virgin olive oil
1 tsp cider vinegar
pinch of salt and pepper

PASTA, MOZZARELLA, CAPERS & SUN-DRIED TOMATOES

For the salad, assemble:

100 g pre-cooked wholewheat fusilli
handful of sun-dried tomatoes, chopped
handful of capers
50 g mini mozzarella balls
bunch of fresh chives, snipped

For the dressing, mix:

1 tbsp extra virgin olive oil
1 tsp balsamic vinegar
pinch of salt and pepper

OMNIVORE

VEGAN ALTERNATIVE
Replace the chorizo with ½ roasted sweet potato

CHORIZO, CROUTONS & MARINATED PEPPERS

For the salad, assemble:

50 g baby spinach
50 g marinated red peppers from a jar, chopped
50 g chorizo, chopped
handful of wholewheat croutons
50 g Pecorino shavings
handful of fresh flat-leaf parsley leaves

For the dressing, mix:

1 tbsp extra virgin olive oil
1 tsp cider vinegar
pinch of salt and pepper

TUNA, CARROT, RED PEPPER & CROUTONS

For the salad, assemble:

handful of rocket
1 carrot, shredded with a julienne peeler
½ red pepper, sliced
50 g tinned tuna (preserved in water), flaked
handful of wholewheat croutons
2 spring onions, sliced
handful of fresh coriander leaves

For the dressing, mix:

2 tbsp mayonnaise
1 tsp dark soy sauce
1 tsp ground ginger

VEGETARIAN ALTERNATIVE

Add 50 g goats' cheese and replace the Nut & Lemon dressing with double cream

PARSNIP, MUSHROOMS, WALNUTS & TRUFFLE CREAM

For the salad, assemble:

1 parsnip, shaved into ribbons with a vegetable peeler
100 g brown mushrooms, sliced
handful of walnuts, chopped
handful of fresh flat-leaf parsley leaves

For the dressing, mix:

1 tbsp truffle-infused olive oil
1 tsp balsamic vinegar
pinch of salt and pepper
2 tbsp Nut & Lemon dressing
(page 26, made with walnuts)

RAW ALTERNATIVE
Replace the mayo and eggs with Raw Pine Nut "Mayo" (page 27)

RED CABBAGE, CARROT, PARSNIP & EGG MAYO

For the salad, assemble:

100 g red cabbage, shredded
½ carrot, shredded with a julienne peeler
½ parsnip, shredded with a julienne peeler
1 tsp poppy seeds

For the dressing, mix:

1 tbsp extra virgin olive oil
1 tsp cider vinegar
pinch of salt and pepper
2 tbsp mayonnaise
1 hard-boiled egg, finely chopped

OMNIVORE

VEGETARIAN
ALTERNATIVE
*Replace the roasted
chicken with more
avocado and some
sun-dried tomatoes*

ROASTED CHICKEN, AVOCADO & CROUTONS

For the salad, assemble:

50 g mixed rocket and lamb's lettuce
½ avocado, chopped
50 g pre-roasted chicken or turkey, sliced
handful of wholewheat croutons
2 spring onions, sliced
50 g Parmesan shavings

For the dressing, mix:

1 tbsp extra virgin olive oil
1 tsp balsamic vinegar
pinch of salt and pepper

MOZZARELLA, ASPARAGUS & CAVOLO NERO

For the salad, assemble:

70 g cavolo nero, chopped (discard the stems)
2 asparagus spears, shaved into ribbons with
  a vegetable peeler
50 g mozzarella, cubed
handful of pine nuts
handful of fresh basil leaves

For the dressing, mix:

1 tbsp extra virgin olive oil
1 tsp balsamic vinegar
pinch of salt and pepper
2 tbsp Classic Pesto (page 25)

VEGAN

VEGETARIAN
ALTERNATIVE
*Add 50 g cottage
or goats' cheese*

CAULIFLOWER, DRIED CRANBERRIES & KALE

For the salad, assemble:

50 g kale, chopped (discard the stems)
100 g cauliflower florets, chopped
½ small red onion, thinly sliced
handful of pistachios
handful of dried cranberries
handful of wholewheat croutons
handful of fresh flat-leaf parsley leaves

For the dressing, mix:

1 tbsp extra virgin olive oil
1 tsp balsamic vinegar
pinch of salt and pepper

RAW

OMNIVORE ALTERNATIVE
Add 50 g roasted chicken or beef, or ham

CAULIFLOWER, HAZELNUTS & DRIED APRICOTS

For the salad, assemble:

50 g mixed baby salad leaves
100 g cauliflower florets, chopped
handful of unsulphured dried apricots,
  chopped
handful of hazelnuts, chopped
handful of fresh flat-leaf parsley leaves

For the dressing, mix:

1 tbsp extra virgin olive oil
1 tsp cider vinegar
pinch of salt and pepper

SMOKED MACKEREL, CAULIFLOWER & ASPARAGUS

For the salad, assemble:

50 g rocket
*2 asparagus spears, shaved into ribbons with
   a vegetable peeler*
60 g cauliflower florets, chopped
50 g smoked mackerel, flaked
handful of pine nuts
handful of fresh flat-leaf parsley leaves

For the dressing, blend together:

1 tbsp extra virgin olive oil
1 tsp lemon juice
pinch of salt and pepper
handful of pumpkin seeds
1 tsp capers

OMNIVORE

VEGAN ALTERNATIVE
Replace the chorizo with smoked tofu

CHORIZO, BLACK QUINOA, ASPARAGUS & EDAMAME

For the salad, assemble:

50 g chorizo, cubed
100 g pre-cooked black quinoa
100 g pre-steamed edamame beans
2 asparagus spears, shaved into ribbons with
  a vegetable peeler
bunch of fresh chives, snipped

For the dressing, mix:

1 tbsp extra virgin olive oil
1 tsp balsamic vinegar
pinch of salt and pepper

CHORIZO, BLACK RICE, PEAS & MARINATED PEPPERS

For the salad, assemble:

100 g pre-cooked black rice
100 g pre-steamed peas
handful of marinated red peppers from a jar
50 g chorizo, sliced
handful of pumpkin seeds
handful of fresh flat-leaf parsley leaves

For the dressing, mix:

1 tbsp extra virgin olive oil
1 tsp balsamic vinegar
pinch of salt and pepper

CRABMEAT, AVOCADO & MARINATED PEPPERS

For the salad, assemble:

60 g rocket
1 avocado, chopped
handful of marinated red peppers from a jar, chopped
50 g cooked crabmeat
bunch of fresh chives, snipped

For the dressing, mix:

1 tbsp extra virgin olive oil
1 tsp lemon juice
pinch of salt and pepper

RAW

PURPLE BROCCOLI, MUSHROOMS & COCONUT FLAKES

For the salad, assemble:

60 g spring greens, shredded
handful of white mushrooms, sliced
100 g purple sprouting broccoli florets, chopped
½ small red chilli, sliced
2 spring onions, sliced
2 tbsp coconut flakes
handful of fresh coriander leaves

For the dressing, mix:

1 tbsp extra virgin olive oil
1 tsp cider vinegar
pinch of salt and pepper

ANCHOVIES, QUAIL EGGS, QUINOA & ASPARAGUS

For the salad, assemble:

50 g spring greens, shredded
50 g pre-cooked white and red quinoa
*1 asparagus spear, shaved into ribbons with
  a vegetable peeler*
3–4 hard-boiled quail eggs, halved
50 g marinated anchovies
bunch of fresh chives, snipped

For the dressing, mix:

1 tbsp extra virgin olive oil
1 tsp cider vinegar
pinch of salt and pepper

OMNIVORE

VEGETARIAN
ALTERNATIVE
*Replace the roasted
turkey with 50 g goats'
cheese*

ROASTED TURKEY & BUTTERNUT SQUASH, & CHICKPEAS

For the salad, assemble:

80 g kale, chopped (discard the stems)
100 g pre-roasted butternut squash, chopped
50 g tinned chickpeas
50 g roasted turkey, thinly sliced
handful of toasted pistachios
handful of dried cranberries
handful of fresh flat-leaf parsley leaves

For the dressing, mix:

1 tbsp extra virgin olive oil
1 tsp balsamic vinegar
pinch of salt and pepper

EGG, ASPARAGUS, CROUTONS & PECORINO

For the salad, assemble:

50 g mixed baby salad leaves
*2 asparagus spears, shaved into ribbons with
a vegetable peeler*
1 hard-boiled egg, cut into wedges
handful of wholewheat croutons
30 g Pecorino, chopped

For the dressing, mix:

1 tbsp extra virgin olive oil
1 tsp balsamic vinegar
pinch of salt and pepper

291

RAW

VEGAN ALTERNATIVE
Replace the sprouted beans with 100 g tinned aduki beans or black-eyed peas

ENOKI MUSHROOMS, AVOCADO & SPROUTED BEANS

For the salad, assemble:

handful of mixed baby salad leaves (e.g. chard, watercress and red oak leaf lettuce)
1 avocado, chopped
50 g enoki mushrooms
handful of sprouted beans (and lentils)

For the dressing, mix:

1 tbsp extra virgin olive oil
1 tsp cider vinegar
pinch of salt and pepper

ROASTED CHICKEN, CANNELLINI BEANS & PEA SHOOTS

For the salad, assemble:

50 g pea shoots or watercress
100 g tinned cannellini or haricot beans
50 g roasted chicken, sliced
handful of dried cranberries

For the dressing, mix:

1 tbsp extra virgin olive oil
1 tsp cider vinegar
pinch of salt and pepper
pinch of saffron threads

APPLE, BROCCOLI, PAK CHOI & ALMONDS

For the salad, assemble:

60 g pak choi or spring greens, shredded
1 apple, chopped
100 g broccoli florets, chopped
handful of almonds
handful of fresh mint leaves

For the dressing, mix:

1 tbsp extra virgin olive oil
1 tsp lemon juice
pinch of salt and pepper
2 tbsp Nut & Lemon dressing (page 26, made with almonds)

BLACK OLIVES, CROUTONS & PARMESAN

For the salad, assemble:

100 g rocket
handful of wholewheat croutons
30 g Parmesan shavings
handful of pitted Niçoise olives
1 tbsp toasted sesame seeds
2 spring onions, sliced

For the dressing, blend together:

1 tbsp extra virgin olive oil
1 tsp tahini
1 tbsp single cream
pinch of salt and pepper

OMNIVORE

VEGAN ALTERNATIVE

Omit the beef and replace the Classic Pesto with Raw Green Pesto (page 25)

ROASTED BEEF, COUSCOUS, ASPARAGUS & KALE

For the salad, assemble:

80 g kale, chopped (discard the stems)
50 g cooked couscous
2 asparagus spears, shaved into ribbons with a vegetable peeler
50 g roasted beef, thinly sliced
handful of fresh flat-leaf parsley leaves

For the dressing, mix:

1 tbsp extra virgin olive oil
1 tsp cider vinegar
pinch of salt and pepper
1 tbsp Classic Pesto (page 25)

VEGAN

VEGETARIAN
ALTERNATIVE
*Add 50 g cottage or
blue cheese*

KALE, NEW POTATOES & BLACK OLIVES

For the salad, assemble:

50 g kale, chopped (discard the stems)
100 g halved and pre-steamed new potatoes
handful of marinated red peppers from a jar
handful of pitted black olives
handful of fresh flat-leaf parsley leaves

For the dressing, mix:

1 tbsp extra virgin olive oil
1 tsp cider vinegar
pinch of salt and pepper

VEGAN

OMNIVORE
ALTERNATIVE
*Add 50 g roasted
chicken or beef,
or smoked ham*

PINTO BEANS, ARTICHOKES & SESAME SEEDS

For the salad, assemble:

50 g rocket
100 g tinned pinto or borlotti beans
handful of grilled, marinated artichoke hearts, chopped
1 tsp toasted sesame seeds
bunch of fresh chives, snipped

For the dressing, mix:

1 tbsp extra virgin olive oil
1 tsp cider vinegar
pinch of salt and pepper
1 tbsp artichoke paste

PESCATARIAN

VEGETARIAN
ALTERNATIVE
Replace the octopus with cheese, such as goats' cheese or feta

OCTOPUS, SUN-DRIED TOMATOES & NEW POTATOES

For the salad, assemble:

50 g rocket
100 g pre-steamed new potatoes
handful of sun-dried tomatoes, chopped
50 g pre-cooked octopus, chopped
handful of fresh flat-leaf parsley leaves

For the dressing, mix:

1 tbsp extra virgin olive oil
1 tsp balsamic vinegar
pinch of salt and pepper

INDEX

ACKNOWLEDGEMENTS

Thanks to my other half, Vera, who started this project with me because of her curiosity about nutrition. Thanks to my dad who is always very proud and supportive even though he hates salads. Thanks to my uncle and aunty who are always there for me. Thanks to all the people who have been there for me all these years, with affectionate support, and even those who have laughed at my little crazy project. Thanks to my colleagues at Discovery, in particular Federico who has tested a lot of the salads, and Judy who has always pushed me forward. Thanks to my agents for being consistently available and resourceful, even with an eight-hour time difference. Thanks to Adrian and the girls at Emerald Street without whom this book wouldn't have happened.